LOVE
and
COURAGE

ROBERT FRANCIS

Copyright @2021 by Mr. Robert Francis

All rights reserved. No part of this book may be reproduced in any form or by any electronic or mechanical means, including information storage and retrieval systems, without permission in writing from the publisher, except by reviewers, who may quote brief passages in a review.

This publication contains the opinions and ideas of its author. It is intended to provide helpful and informative material on the subjects addressed in the publication. The author and publisher specifically disclaim all responsibility for any liability, loss or risk, personal or otherwise, which is incurred as a consequence, directly or indirectly, of the use and application of any of the contents of this book.

WORKBOOK PRESS LLC
187 E Warm Springs Rd,
Suite B285, Las Vegas, NV 89119, USA

Website:	https://workbookpress.com/
Hotline:	1-888-818-4856
Email:	admin@workbookpress.com

Ordering Information:
Quantity sales. Special discounts are available on quantity purchases by corporations, associations, and others.
For details, contact the publisher at the address above.

Library of Congress Control Number:
ISBN-13:   978-1-956017-45-8 (Paperback Version)
           978-1-956017-46-5 (Digital Version)

REV. DATE: 24/08/2021

ROBERT FRANCIS

CONTENTS

LOVE ELEVATION 1

QUALITIES SHINES 4

BLESSINGS 7

IN TOUCH OF EMOTIONS 9

GOOD JUDGEMENT 13

FORGIVENESS 16

DIVINE JOURNEY 18

POWER 19

WISDOM POWER 21

COURAGE 24

SPIRITUAL ENERGIES 26

SECURITY IN LIFE 27

ENGAGING IMAGES OF CHARACTERS 30

CHARACTER CHANGES 32

MIND AND SOUL INSPIRATIONS 36

LIMITATIONS 37

STRENGTH OF LIGHT 42

LEGACY TO YOU 45

AGONY WITH INTEGRITY 48

ABILITIES OF CONFIDENCE 52

LEGACY OF THE DIVINE	56
RIGHTFUL GROUND	61
SPIRITUAL BENEFICIARY	63
SERENITY AND POWER	67
MYSTIC ELEMENTS	71
UNITY IN REFLECTION	72
REVELATIONS	74
DELUSIONS	75
LOYALTY IS STRENGTH	77
GENEROSITY	80
INDEPENDENCE IN RIGHTEOUSNESS	82
WISDOM POWER	84
LOVE AS ONLY COMMITMENT	86
SPIRITUAL APPRECIATIONS	89
ONE AND ONLY TRUE MASTER	90
A PRAYER	92
OUR JOURNEY	93
LOVE CONQUERS	95
HONOR!	96
FACING REALITY	97

Love and Courage

When you walk along the border of love! You will see no changes, but elevation. You will see no artificial, but natural. You will see no pretending heart! But a heart that is touched by the indwelling spiritual power of love; or to say, by the power of the Almighty God, the Creator of all living things! The reflection of love mystifies our understanding in accordance with wisdom. So we could see our Imperfection of who we are, and who we can become!

As to the proof and Evidence of this divine power! We are to behold with our eyes which signals our minds the evidence which this divine power has created! The open sky, the Earth in its substance that grows the trees, fruits and food and other

Living things that walk the face of this earth, all these things are evident to the divine truth! God Almighty, subject of life himself! The whole world has Him in every sense of the word. His life forces the Holy Spirit, which dwell among the living! What then when we go through these agony and pain. Some have the chance of enjoying life! From the time they were born, all through to the time they died. What about those who rise and fall, and for some who never rise? But always struggling until they died? Would you say that those that have better convenience of life are better than those who struggle all through until they died? I would disagree if you say 'yes!' Life is the most essential power and gift upon the face of this Earth! And everyone has the chance or opportunity to live it, until they die, are those who came to be witnesses, to see this beautiful natural earth. And we all made and make decisions! Some of us are satisfied with decision making. And some are not satisfied!

Some of us need a second chance. In fact, we all need a second chance; because we are not perfect! We all have our short comings, through the existence of life. The breath that we breathe is of no better quality, between the rich and the poor, or any other nations! The breath of life is coming from, one true divine source. A source that is perfect even, beyond all comprehension of humans, and all nations! There is no faculty or power of the mind from any human that can be compared to the mystification of the Almighty; the true divine power of the creator! If we could just connect with each other on a positive level! To feel the energy from one to the other! We could spread a spiritual revolutionary power force, across the face of this earth! Every man would be touch beyond the extended divinity by experiencing what the power of unity is all about! It would be His glory resting upon our head!

If we could isolate ourselves momentarily and individually, in connection within ourselves! We will hear the answers to all the questions from within. You would know and realize that the truth is your friend, which will always set your heart, soul and mind free. Living with and by the truth, will build your confidence, broaden your courage, and keep your endurance through the dark times of your goings. Remember, your power of mind is weak, when you are not entrusted to the truth. Or when we are not resting on that divine promise, which never leaves us until death?

What happens when you start to face the hard times? When all the disappointment begins to happen! When you don't know how to face the issues, or in what ways to handle it! When you feeling overwhelming, tears running down your face, having no insight or strength of hope! Momentarily, is as if your life and opportunity is slipping out of your hands. When you overreact, that's the time when things get out of control. What do you do then? This is part of the situation, when someone says, 'calm down', It is to find the courage to get deep within yourself! And to understand the experiences you are going through, one has the opportunity of equality, freedom and power for soul searching! To see the right from wrong, to make a conscious decision! Through the midst of the storm, we have to find peace or calmness to build confidence. Let's seek for loyalty with courage, by bringing out the strength and reaction as a starting point for resolution. When you connect with yourself on the spiritual side of life! You will be enabled to connect with others. More so, characteristically relating to someone, the way you would relate to God. In the true sense of his divine plans!

LOVE ELEVATION

Love as the power of life. In so knowing about love, all things are possible! Through the understanding of the divine words, with actions! Almighty God is the true sense of the Word. For in the beginning was the Word, and the Word is God. And the same which is the word, is the spirit of life, was formed flesh and dwelt upon this Earth, among men.

In my view, the heart of love has no blemish, because the very soul of the Almighty is pure and clean. Love is the greatest power, or blessing untouchable through the wisdom and understanding, in the eyes of the Most High God! The very mystifying touch of his spiritual mind of Love has one clothing, like a leopard skin which cannot change! Love as one dignifying direction, a direction which has no limitation. But the tendency is from the spiritual to the physical! Because the Lord God has transcended his Image into mankind! So we can feel the touch of his presence and blessings. We are one of his moving, active forces, of which his love broadens the way. Where the power of the Father's immortal being is concern, there is no limitation.

His life is everywhere, in the cattle of all kind, the birds of all kinds, creeping things, fishes of the sea of all kinds! Love will not and cannot disappear, if so, where would love go? Or where would He go, if He should disappear? The very aspect of Him, his character is folded up in one ball of His promises. He will never leave us nor forsake us. As for you who are out there, please hold to His promises. You can also say, he will never leave me! God will never dismiss his world out of existence. For God is a part of the existence and the head of the existence. So why would he turn from His promises? His love which contains, justice, peace, mercy, forgiveness, understanding and wisdom! The very spiritual character of his image would be meaningless. And it is impossible for all this creation to crumble. Because the Almighty is the possibility of life, and of our lives! We live and feel his energy through our veins. He has the power over life and death, and we are very important in his master plans. We join with Jehovah, to carry out his spiritual legacy. That good will always overcome evil. Good will not and will never be defeated by evil. So therefore for the soldiers who are ready to fight for Righteousness! They will have a reward, and so is the same for the soldiers who stand up for evil.

What I'm saying here is that there are different characteristics within our Integrities. And we must pass on these different characteristics to generations, so that we inherit the power of love as we journey along in Life.

I tell you a story about rewarding from the things we do. I was working with an East Indian over the years! On and off, during all these times. Honestly, I always looking for job with more pay. Driving semi-truck or Tractor trailers! And I mean, I need money for the family. My salary could hardly sustain the family. It just from hand to mouth! For five years my wife doesn't have a steady job. And so I was shouldering all the responsibilities. In this case having a full time job, I was looking for a part time to fill in some of the gaps! That how I ended up working for this East Indian guy! But I never let go the thoughts of looking for a better job that will pay more money, than what I'm getting for full time. So I begin to experiencing when pay day came around. It takes me some two days to get paid. In some pay days, I had my rent to pay and other bills. I took action looking for other job. I was succeeding, I found a job; this company is on my resume. So the East Indian knew, I was looking for another job. But I didn't want him to know I got a job. Time set for my orientation! The very day to start on my orientation, the East Indian ask me to work for him! That day earlier in the morning before the orientation begins. I mean, this guy is a very nice guy, it was just the pay period was messing things up. I couldn't say to him straight off the bat. That I got a new job, and I can't work for you anymore. It felt like I would be damaging the trust between the both of us. So I agree to the job, and made matters worse. When the hour came for the orientation, I had to confess a little to him. His response was, ok, on my surprise after the orientation class. The truck was gone, half hour drive from where my car was. Took me three hours walk back to the car. Because I was not straight with him telling him the truth, of the whole situation! In other words, the more a person is honest within oneself. Is the better communication will be, for everyone! The energy of life mystified every one spiritually. Love never fails!

Love and Courage

Love to the world, and for the human race. Kids should grow with confidence, to build a better world of tomorrow!

QUALITIES SHINES

Every living soul should know that life is a journey. And always end up with its destiny. Let's take a moment to reflect on the wild side concerning the infrastructures that we build which we name: roads, streets, Avenues, Lanes and highways. But these entire infrastructures were built for us as human beings to travel on. To journey on, to find our destination literally and to share connections. It is also a symbol to our spiritual journey! Sometimes we are on the same road, journeying along the way, but we are not touching down on the same destiny ground. One will stop before the other, and the decisions we make brings us to a stop sign, or turns us off the pathways! And we are rewarded according to the impact of the paths of our lives' circumstances! If not all. Is it the impact of how we were brought up by our families? From one generation to the other! When we were in our childhood, experiencing Love and confidence! Our parents handed over to us the tools of knowledge, understanding and wisdom. And don't forget first and foremost top priority the teaching of spiritual growth! How to love and understand the Almighty's power! Who created all things naturally! Remember when we were babies before we grew up, and we intended to follow or to keep up to those wise words of instructions which were taught by our parents, and family friends? Memories will never be forgotten by the strength and substances, with the courage through our lives' experiences. For the best part, if not most of us, will bring this life changing experiences over to our children? So that the journey of life we take, result in our good destiny. Never-the-less there are some of us who never have the perfect upbringing per se! And they face their rise and fall, ups and down and learn through their agony and pain, in tough times! And through the rain, they turn out to be shining gold. The mystery of love, works wonders as God Almighty mystified their minds with courage and strength.

We should never allow ourselves to lie down and die or to keep crying saying it's too hard to take the pain! Without doing anything. Think about the vehicle that breaks down on the side of the road. And the owner leaves it there, and goes for help or to get a mechanic to have the vehicle repaired! I say, that person wanted to keep going. He or she doesn't want to keep stuck forever. And that's the open door of chances, the Creator has allowed in our lives. So when we are broken down like a broken car, we should rise up for the repairing of ourselves! And the spiritual strength which he gives us, will handle any given situation in our lives. We can't afford for the devil to come into our lives to weaken us with his deceptions of lies, confusing our minds and leading us into the dark! We then, will not see where to walk but will be as a human race, struggling through confusion and pain. Throughout our whole lives became chronic strugglers through hardship, as we constantly relax our minds, because we don't know what to do. Courage has left us, because of the negatives and delusions that sink within our hearts, as we lose confidence, in Love and peace of mind. We are losing the full image of our Legacy, which was given to us from the Almighty Creator! The devil spread his character in the heart of politicians of mankind. As they rap us into a blanket of foolishness, keeping us Quiet and comfortable. The world made their vain lives very exciting like a rushing wind diluting the value of wisdom. Causing future generations to value the world message of excitement instead and this is being sent to generations! We are not redirecting or redefining ourselves to find the true sense of life's meaning. We are in a confused state of mind at various levels! Doing the opposite of the right and light, as to the wrong and the dark! In the spiritual connection terms, they call the night day, and the light is dark before their eyes. They call righteousness boring, and wickedness they call exciting. The world sees the security of life, to be insecurity, and destructions became limitless, in our lives. They said we should have protection with literal weapons. Which are the weapons of destruction? But you see, all these things have a meaning. Because the person whose vehicle is broken down on the side of the road in the process of the journey! Now knows what was going on with the vehicle. The solution is to get it repaired. So is our lives, on other level so is the spiritual level.

Robert Francis

This is one of the examples we are facing in our daily lives. We should redirect our part, when there is a mistake. How would we know the temperature of the heat, if we don't feel it? Or to acknowledge how cold the winter is, so we can prepare ourselves. God knows best for our lives, and he wants to give us all we need!

BLESSINGS

Because out of the abundant of his Love. His discernment, and Loyalty, justice, peace and happiness! And the list goes on; the Creator is saying he is not running a rat race. With evilness or with the devil! He said this is where I stand, in the power of Righteousness. I am the conqueror for everything in life. And God shines his own light, through wisdom we can recognized him. By the will of him, we can find true happiness. There is a soul searching that equally allows every men and women, boys and girls; to an everlasting Creator, who is the source of life? So don't let delusion take you out of place anymore. Because the consequence is there honestly to pay! Love is the get-away, Love is the freedom, and Love is over bound with courage. That's spiritual strength, which we always needed for our lives; to reign in victory unto prosperity! Character changes, verses true light of peace, from the divine power above. He is our connection, our only source of happiness. There are no struggles, agony and pain or catastrophe: That anyone is going through, that can't be overcome. Or to be heal by the hands of the true heavenly divine source! All things are possible, through the strength of our minds; when the trust goes to God Almighty! When the watch smith made the watches or the clocks! He or she done their researching first, before they make all these time keeping. He knows all these attachment, for putting these clocks together. So when it's broken, the watch smith can repair it. What about the builder of the house, he or she can repair the house? Whatever may happen to the house, it can be repair. So therefore we have the true divine source of a true mystifying power to repair our hearts and souls, when they're broken! **Because he is the true living master!** And the Creator of all living things! Knowing all of this with full knowledge and awareness. We should join his army to be true soldiers. Fighting individually and collectively, fight for the weak and the poor in spirit. And your reward will, lying up to a place that will never be touch. From everlasting to everlasting! The pure in heart shall understand through wisdom. How to walk into true divine fulfillment. For the strength of our minds, hands and feet; is coming from the heavenly reach! These are the days, when we need a source of strength, power and true confident. To step through the darkness of evilness. Breaking down delusions and all negative approaches in our lives.

While there is life, there are experiences to gain. But you must always remember that life, love and courage, is more than death. Because Love never dies, but live to serve in strength to humanity. So where do we go from here, in all the thickness of all pages of life. As we may know on one side in life! There is sweetness, happiness and beauty never end. On the other side you have! Darkness, delusion, confusion, destruction and pollution. Causing struggles of life in misunderstanding, lack of communications. Revengeful to each other, reflecting action of hatred. We are not in agreement of the truth! Psychological war fare under the sun. Is not many realized that the little strength we have. We should make the best of us with it. Ignites the energy of positivity in our circle. So we could feel and see the radiant around us spreading. Only love that conquers; and hatred divides us in all sense of the word. There is a sense of connection within the soul of humanity, so we can have an outreach of the heart. By conditioning ourselves to the depth of knowledge, understanding and wisdom; it will keep us in the circle of unity! There is a spirit that which works in between our vision. To see situations and circumstances which as connects the ego on a personal and collective level. And will keep us grow towards prosperity; in the benefit for our families. Every man should keep his house in Order, likewise his own heart; by lifting our soul through love and courage. Within the level and condition of integrity in our lives, communications are not just talking! It is to keep ourselves connected, as we dialogue. Which means we are on the same page, with our thoughts and feelings? We should value ourselves as importantly as anyone else. For each person, is of the cosmos gift of this creation. The lives of humanity have the rest of this timeless time; to get deeper with this divine source of creations. Has we allowed our opportunities and connections with love and courage!

IN TOUCH OF EMOTIONS

Has he opening a new world and a new journey, on holy ground. As we plead more for love, his love. Our connections are of his connection in the surroundings of our lives. We should come together and break down Obstacles and barriers, from around us. And not to creates barriers and Obstacles in front of us. We are just only human, who could encounter in the shadow of happiness; love, prosperity and peace! When we cause some of our family into a nasty situation. We should get back ourselves on the water! And pull that family member out of situation. Because no one is an island, mentally, spiritually and emotionally. We all should lean on each other's shoulders. For strength and support! Because our lives came from one true divine destiny. We are flesh and bone of humanity, one human race family. Flesh of our flesh, bone of our bones. Disregarding the colors of skins, eyes and height. What we as human race must regard, is communication in love and courage. From the navel string of a pregnant mother! The baby was nurtured from the food the mother eats. So is our spiritual life and journey with the almighty one. Full connections with the true mystical divine source of creation! What I'm also saying, is that we will never see the power of Love. If we don't show some kind of action, that the power of love, Action. Life is lasting and everlasting, when we show courage, love, honesty and loyalty. In this world we are depending on one another in the circle of life; through the will and power of the heavenly father! Who connect within our minds through the spirit of life? It doesn't matter the colors, class, or creed. It doesn't matter cultures or positions, whether high or low. What I'm saying, we should not systematically encounter love, with pride. Or to differentiate others with pride! Saying who is better than the other. No, it's one love, one soul, one destiny. We all journey through circumstances, but the destination is there for us all. Characteristically accordingly you have your reward; but no one is better than the other, we are one creation. Almighty God is Love! Can we see the breath of life breathe inside our bodies? Are we starting to choose who is to be forgiven for the wrongs? Differently from what circumstances that should be forgiven for? Remember when situations happen! We are still link with each other's. When the victims in their pain and sorrows, the confronter of the victim. Still feel some emotion of that cause, no one is disconnected. In the circle of life, we are family, human families. When Cain kills his brother Able, do you think he has any remorse of his act? I know he did, but he couldn't bring back the life of Able. And also in his anger, his response was very presumptuous with God. So curse was the reward for his actions. When husband and wife having discordance. Whichever side the misunderstanding is coming from! Or who-so-ever done the wrong deeds, regarding what the circumstances are. As human nature, we intent to walk away from each other's! But by doing so, we are only discrediting the powers of Love, Loyalty and courage? Within the circumstances we should have the ability of good judgments for our intimate and social relationship; so we can see the light, in the strength of forgiveness. Resolves situation peacefully and gracefully. Because the ball is not in our court, on our behalf. But the ball is in our court by his behalf! Because, he the Almighty Father is the head of Righteousness? Some of us are very strong above certain circumstances. Which is to say, I will never say and do that to hurt he or she? So why do I have to get hurt and stays with the relationship? First that's pride, and type of pride I'm talking about, is the type which goes with prejudice! Because what I'm seeing here, I am too good to give to someone like you: this quality of relationship. And looking on the situation you allowed! Look what happening, between the both of us. How could you, I would never do this to you! Now I say, after you vent out all of that anger, pain and disappointment. You should think about the values, your Relationship reflects. Where are the good things? which cause your romance and love? Keeping both of you going strong, before this disappointment came along. Are you going to flush out all the good memories? Because of one terrible thing happen to your good quality relationship? I say forgiveness; will give you greater quality strength: far more of what you were thinking of, through these trials of life. Only when we open our minds to the realities before our eyes.

What we need is his divine presence! And naturally shows your sweet, sweet smiling each day. As to the rising of the sun to the going down! In the present of the divine promises, as we look within. And hear the conscience speaks with full confident and power. We should set a border around our humanness. And focus more on our consciousness! Human pride trip in, thinking more or less; I am better then you in that way of life! How could you think of other human being that way? Because of the negative force of pride anchors our minds! How could you think that you are the better person, then he or she! So in conclusion you were thinking about that all along, that you are the better person! Shame on you, how you value yourself before the highest living God. Yes, the master of love and life, because you are nothing without him. For the life that's in your body is not yours. And the love you use to connect with each other's, is not yours. Take away all of that, what do you have to show for yourself? Nothing! So why when someone done you wrong; it becomes so hard in the process to share the power of forgiveness? That was allowed for us to use in any given circumstances, why are you holding back? As if it is your power, and you are not a victim in the path way of the devil plans. When you forgive someone, you add and allow more power of light to your life. Because the God of creation of all living; he already put all these plans in place! Or access of these tools; like loyalty, forgiveness and Love, joy, peace and happiness and prosperity! Through his divine wisdom, knowledge with understanding? It is the connection through communications level for all mankind; to find resolutions within our hearts and soul; as life combines us in a progressive journey!

When we do good things for others. It's because we are keeping connecting with the divine power of the highest, Jehovah God. As we pray each day for deliverance for life; and the lives of families and your family! We will see different changes in our modes, beautiful reflections in our circle of life! It's the way are in tune with the mystified strength of our lives; whose grace and mercy is abundantly towards us! As his love enriches our lives of his many blessings. Only when we surrender our lives to his will, by saying. Most righteous and eternal master, you are the greatest master that so ever lived? And in, so ever sure in faith, hope, courage, in mighty and power! Above life, and of life itself! You are the remedy maker in every given situation. You mighty Lord stand up like priest, and like a king. And like servant to served your people! Like soldier to protect your chosen people! And we are your children who called on thy name daily. You enrich us with your Integrity that can't be broken. Moreover, when our emotions are broken, and despair is endless. When it seems like there is no resolution, for agony and pain. Your healing power brings sunshine, through the rain. There is not anything that is hard for you to do. But everything connects with the heart and soul and mind. Like the father, son and Holy Spirit!

GOOD JUDGEMENT

So after you came to such a great acknowledgement about God? The living God! What there else to do, he is one of the greatest revelation could ever reveals; to you, on the way about consciousness in life. He is not just happening, he is the purpose for our existence; who is the mystified power, the one true living God! Who inspired our hearts to these acknowledgements, has we engage our everyday living through his mercy? Wherein we begin to see how important it is to reflect upon him! For he is the key person of our lives! We have to begin to reset for our very best, with a new format!

We should start to reshuffle life equation, on a different level; and this would be a blessing, and a gift for our lives. And where courage would inspire the vision of love! Never under-estimate the power of what Love can do for your life! Love esteems Loyalty, over view eternity; and make no second thought about that. Love is a compassion to our soul! Love brings out all the light and vision to our lives; in the open for everyone to see! And we should know that the devil hate righteousness. And refused to do what is right. Love causes us naturally to be happy, without looking back at the pass with regrets! We got to understand this, that love carries the full package in everything for our lives! How about courage, strength, justice, peace, happiness, prosperity, Loyalty, goodness and good vision with integrity. All of these facets of Love and many more in the package. So you see my friends, after you come to this side of the river, of acknowledgement. There should be no turning back from the consciousness of life. If you slip, don't stay there keeping slipping away. If so, that's a sign that your spiritual consciousness; is taking a run through the back door, of spiritual darkness! Simple means you are focusing on the Locust. And not on the power of wisdom with great standing of vision to life. As the Holy Spirit reveals, when the people lost visions they begin to perish. Their hearts and minds thinking of the negative; and not of the positive. And we all know that the positive elevates us to higher heights. Positivity holds you in gravity; never lose your dignity, or integrity! As we surface along with prosperity, it is the hands of spirituality, keeps us on the way from deformities.

Hold tight my people, for the strength of sincerity, it's a legacy from the Almighty. And a gift of God to men for eternity. So please stop the negativity and holds to positivity; because it quenches you thirst, when you are thirsty. Don't give up, stand with God! And face the fight against the enemy. And you will come out victoriously. And let that be your testimony, because love and praise of Jehovah, is of good quality. We should have great standing of hope and faith. In the creator, who is of all creation! And step by steps we will purge our hearts on our journey to our destiny. His will is in our lives. Just keep this in mind, that this life is not ours but his. He gave life to us, so we can have used it to glorify his power. In all his will of righteousness. Hold this thought strong to your heart, that's, a prayer a day, will keep the Devil away. Don't focus on the mistake you made. But on the good you can do for yourself, and for others. For I say this to you. If you recognized the wrongs or mistakes, and sincerely ask for forgiveness. Worry not, for the God of justice and righteousness. Who is on your side, knows your very heart and Intension. Be not afraid of those who jump to conclusions, and judge your name. That never to say, your character of who you are, in the name of the Most High of Israel. Keep steadfast in your good deeds, in prayer and meditation. That is your medication of protection, through his will and power.

When you have God by your side. You should smile with great confident. Because who can withstand the spiritual power of the Almighty? He is in your corner, and he will never turn his back, against his words. The very words are who he is. Why would God turn against himself? And gave us his words to prove of who he really is. Knowing that his words are the very presence of his character. And as he faces us with this questions asking. Have you ever seeing the words of the Heavenly Father changes? When we have love and forgiveness in our heart! We can accomplish so many things, or overcome so many obstacles. Because working with these two power plates releases, and overcome. Your burden and stress, anxiety, pressure and weight you carry on your mind. Let's make some good sense of this, forgiveness, as the power to allow us. To deletes the wrongs or pain we cause to someone. Or someone cause us.

FORGIVENESS

Love and forgiveness take away your sadness. And redirect your thoughts, just by letting go of the evil thoughts. Total resentment, and make ourselves anew! It's not much of an easy task, as the word speak of forgiveness. But as you let go your humanness. And listen step by step to God holy words of righteousness. You would be amaze, of what there left to see. We know time worked miracles in our lives! When we allow the will of his majesty, to cause us to see reality. As the writer said, every thousand step, start first with one. There is a beginning for accomplishment. And there is a journey, to see your destiny. But love never fails the Almighty! God has nowhere to go from his people. He can't hide, but to stay vivid in the heart and soul, mind and body. He has no challenger to take him out, from his throne of righteousness. Or to break him down from his kingdom power. When you found someone who is so awesome as such! What sense would it make you not to trust in him? And to ask him for things or to follow his example in life. The father's hands are blessed and prosperous; His intensions are to be humble, for the weak and the poor. So let's promise never to change from his directions. Sometimes we talk about the truth. Which is the divine cultural roots of life? It's a reflection towards peace and happiness; no matter how many wrongs you have done. Once, you surrender to the power of truth, that you were wrong. And ask for the gift of forgiveness, and accept that gift with diligence. We will find our way back to peace of mind. Which will enable us, to focus on the way, the journey of life? We all should know that we are on a divine journey. Our lives always facing spiritual obstacles in every step of the way! Therefore, be in full accordance with the conscience of our mind? Take a little meditation to refocus each day of your life! So we can overcome barriers and obstacles, which try to bump us off our journey. By holding confident in hope of the divine promises. The fatherhood of righteousness, the security to our destiny! Please, let's come to this acknowledgement, that it is only one divine might, and strength. Throughout this creation, courage, to represent the motherhood. Which is righteousness, the energy of holiness? Stand up with a tension and intention. To share the importance, the breath that we breathe through our nostril. It is potentially proven that the creator is in the midst of our lives! His mercy love and courage is with us, he assured us that he will always be with us. The heavenly father said, I am always there with you and to all human races. To give you courage and love, in this way you will keep connects with me, having no doubts. So you can carry through peacefully with life journey. He hammers down his hand to say. I am your treasure, and you're my lost pearl that I couldn't find. While I was with you in the eyes of grace, mercy and truth. My sheep, and my chosen children, I live so that you all might live! So surrender your heart and soul, to the true divine one of Israel. And not your vanity life or your garments, by disregarding your true destiny! And living among the steel bars of this world. Thinking that you are in true accord finding happiness, you are making a huge mistake. As the proverbs states, anywhere a man is. His shadow is there with him, but he can't hold his shadow. So is the world today among the people, but the people can't hold the system of the world. But there is a hand sincerely reaching out, to every heart and soul. With a sincere divine guarantees, wherein every person can catch that hand. Don't let hard times get us down! Or to distract us from the truth. Or from the freedom in life! Because there is a way to build our spiritual muscles! In faith and hope through his eternal power! Love from his majesty is here to connect us and to keep us! As one human race, and not to be afraid of negative forces. You see my friends; we are the sheep of his pastures. And he is our master, sometimes when there is no grass in the pastures. Humble still and look to him, as the provider and the guider! We are here to rest our head upon his shoulder. Has he felt our pain and agony! And his love from one to the other brings us comfort. What more we need when we surround by a mighty power; he is the giant who defend us in any given situation.

DIVINE JOURNEY

That causes us not, to destroy our lives! The discerner is the true positive life force. That defended us within the ability of our knowledge, wisdom and understanding. Or (power-standing) through the will of his holy spiritual character! We were all created uniquely under the visions of his purpose, to do his will. Only Jehovah reign from everlasting to everlasting, in his kingdom power.

The good book says, for God so love the world. That he gave his only begotten son. That who-so-ever believeth in him should be unhappy! Ashamed, frustrated, feeling condemnation, feeling lost without the gift of forgiveness. No. God in his holy spiritual character said that we will have everlasting life. And what I personally got from this statement. Is first, his holy spirit of life will comfort us in all ways. By bringing peace and contentment, through the word of wisdom! Understanding his confirmation, as we know it very well! And that clarity is the very key to life! And all of his riches we receive, when we trusted and believed. In his holy kingdom power! There is a strong saying, show me your company, and I can tell who you are. It is the company you engage with, is an influence to your lives! Whether good or bad, the choice is yours. But if you choose the good company! You well influence by the goodness and righteousness of life destiny. And this is a confirmation to his promises, to all human races. That whatsoever a man sows, so shall he reap. Because it is seal and sign by the hands of the Almighty. That from his heart to your heart! The connection and awareness of your knowledge to his.

POWER

And a step to the door of courage. It's the light of true charity; from a mystifying majesty surround you! It's the holy ground part way; It makes sense to walk in the right part of life! It's a sense of honor and courage and integrity towards life prosperity. In high places, and power against the human race. But (Jah) or Jehovah also said that there is no power that form against you shall not prosper.

For example, a man who love his son so much. He would do anything to guide and protect his son from all dangers of life. So first he will teach his son how to understand the words, and what is right from wrong. Sometimes stand by to see how he will handle situations around himself. In other words, be observant of his spiritual engagement. How he would handle himself through obstacles of life. What are his morals towards immoralities, keep in mind that his father is closer to him into every given situation? He always there to fill him with the morals of life! This is one of the advantage to the son, if he is an obedient son. Then in most cases he will invites his father attention. To the things, that he is about to do before he begins to do it. Because he wants to be certain of the right thing, he is about to do. You see, obedience is part of courage. To have and to show mercy is part of courage. To show forgiveness is courage. In my view forgiveness is like open the window of your heart. To allow fresh air of Love and righteousness to blows through your heart! By refreshing your mind with peace and contentment, between you and that someone! In the very thoughts of our life journey. Even though you are forgiving that someone, you also forgive yourself. Can you see that transcending richness of blessings! The father has given his son, so unto us his legacy of eternal righteousness. Which is the root of life that bears fruits, between God and the human race? Through his moral principles, the charity from the father to the son. So is the Love from the son to the human race. Love is free when the heart of the human race received it freely.

Don't contaminate or corrupt or cause yourself, to be contagious with foolishness or infatuation! All of this will only discredit your happiness and peace of mind. Naturally, the quality of life is joy, peace and happiness. When you are not in that directions of faith. When the storms come's and the furies come's as on obstacles in your life! You won't get through it, because the common ground of righteousness; wasn't your first choice to life destiny! Which means from the beginning of your life? You are not recognizing your surroundings, you weren't adopting through the process of life principles; for the goodness to your heart, to be strong and courageous! By standing up for moral principles! You see in this world are fill with contamination, and contagious with immoralities. So we have to stand up with the openness of our hearts, to see the truth! So we may find strength making the right decisions, for the benefit of our lives.

WISDOM POWER

Don't attach yourself to inferiority, badness, deficiency and imperfection. Even though we are imperfect, comparing to the holiness of God righteousness! But don't attach to madness. Attach to the wisdom and understanding from above, and you will find love. We should honestly feel the good energy within ourselves! So we could share this evidence of positivity! Within us as people, a creation that was created positive from a positive hands and mind! From this prospective of creation, let's attach or engage ourselves. To this natural timeless beauty from the hands of the Almighty from earth to Zion! The gift of legacy to all human races, his heart is beyond the purest of purity? He stands alone in the holy of the holiest. He paved the way for his creation. He gave us the tools for the time throughout our endeavors. Whatever challenges we are facing. Whatever power shapes our way, he allows us to have a one to one chat with him. Has we humble ourselves in connection unto him. Our lives will never be a regrets or disappointment from the father of creation. Or the Lord of our integrities! Life is beyond what men could ever imagine. When we think back over the generations thousands of years. Up to the time of this generation, we should realize how many things we have discovered. In the world of civilization within the advance, I must say. There are many more to discover in this civilized world. Question to all of what will be discover of this world civilization. If everything was to be discovered in one day! What you think would have happen to this world of today? It's very impossible for one-day discovery. Because creation did not in the existence on that level. For throughout the lives of the human race they learn stage by stage under different level. Circumstance in their lives. But just imagine if it was possible. I think there would be more corruptions in a wide range in society. Because of the deep advancement among men, in this advance world of society! And of such advancement would be coming from the same source as it is now. And always will be, but there is a limited portion. That has cast upon every future generation to uplift the mark of civilization! In all parts of the human faculties! But don't forget that with this one roll, or ball. As to say, the nature of life, the breath of life is in its power. That which exposed unto the negative vibes! Which we call sin. That which we were educated by calling human nature? The human races have side-track in their own selfishness in actions and thoughts!

By satisfied their feelings; thinking that they are bringing justification, to the works of their righteousness. But as a result it's the rewarding of destruction. Every man is trying to Walk; in their own kingdom power. Saying that they can, and wants to do what their mind as them set out to do! This is the length, depth, and heights of where the civilized world has reached in its power. But according to the spiritual contents of the human journey! From generations to generations, upon the spiritual source and inspiration. From the Creator who created the heaven and the earth! The stars, moon, and sun, he is the source of nature, to all living things. And he has inspired men to unfold the knowledge of truth to the human race! As to say we the generations, has up lifting the educational standard of knowledge to his righteousness. So that we the generations will find; Joy, peace and happiness of one's life! It's a link to find better judgments of honesty, humbleness and loyalty. To the hearts of men! In whom the Creator has shown justice from the heart of his mercy, to the whole universe.

But as we describe the civilized world of society in their pumps and pride! For the head source from which cometh these kingdom rulers. God the Creator of all living things; has described these civilized societies. As Babylonian kingdom earthly rulers! Jehovah Most High has been describing the head of these societies' rulers as Satan. The Devil, master of evilness, and deception! The transformer of lies and manipulation in corruptions. He would, if he could to turn all human beings heart up sided down. And to let the entire earth crumbles under his feet. Through his master deceptions of his kingdom ruler ship! But with the honor and glory to the Most High God Almighty, in his righteousness! In his hands he has the power over good and evil. And he is using the power of good to overcome evil. And that's another bonus of salvation towards justice, peace and harmony. It's a gift from his love, as we learn to nourish, cherish and nurtured life. By loving our Neighbors, as we are to loves ourselves! And through this channel we learn more of the will of God. Having said this; within the present of life, how can we say that God is not with us? {Because the very presence of life}, is the very presence of Gods holy spirit! Why would we say, we don't have access to Gods glory? Regardless what may be our deformities, physical or spiritual? The grace of the Most High, his love is the key and strength to our victory throughout our life journey. How beautiful when we get to our destiny. It will be as bright as seven times fold as the sun light by day. That's says to our connection in God Almighty was very good! We all know when we hear the knocking at our heart door towards righteousness. As to say, when our conscience speaks. It is for us to identify his voice, and it should be glorious to open the door. And received his blessings and the power of his healings. God in all his characters (facets), he has prepared himself in all of these conditions. His righteousness is just for you and me! There is no other energy we can feel from the Lord our God. But the energy of righteousness! Such as peace, love, joy and loyalty, in the eyes of hope and faith of his happiness! His legacy is prepared for us here on Earth, and in the Heaven's. If we paid attention to peace, our barriers of strength and power; will not be thrown down. God gave us all the courage we need to walk through the mountains, valleys and fires. Through the calm, through the storms! The charity of God cut through the thickest walls of hard times.

COURAGE

His courage; hope and faith in his love! Will reveals the greatest of our lives. We are facing so many obstacles in life each day. That the cross we bear, the experiences we facing! This is the test we taste to rise triumphantly, and victoriously. It is the joy we find, as we experiencing the journey through life. We are refining and redefining ourselves through the journey of our lives. Yes, I say yes. It is possible to find confidence in ways of circumstances. Confidence is a treat, God has opened unto us! So we can enjoy each step we make in any given situations. Knowing within ourselves that the Most High Jehovah is our creator! Who is everything in natural nature? He always by our side to guide and protect us! Throughout the ways of life given challenges? Be of no fear the father is everywhere.

If you wish, may I take the time to remind us? That the breath that the creator breathes through our nostrils. Is the life of his holy image? That when he said let's make man in our own image. That the breath which he breathes in our nostrils! Is the image of his character and his wellness! His glory, wisdom, knowledge understanding the depth of his very Love! God is sharing the Master plan of his legacy with you and his life! It's very essential to the light of his glorious and authentic moment upon earth among mankind. The righteousness of the Almighty one is unlike no other! And it is the only way and direction for life to have honor and power. The fullest of life is through the Majesty of the Almighty with that everlasting reflection! His divinity rules over all the existing planets, where life force nature is concern; without Question! These are the steps we taken through the eyes of courage.

By finding the strength rewarding peace and happiness, with God and in God! Considering the dark times around our lives! The struggling we encounter with each day. When we rise up in the morning from our slumber? Showing appreciation to life, by giving thanks for his divine presence. Considering the danger of this contagious pollution of negative energies, among the innocent! Among the weak who is trying to be strong! These thick dark painful struggles we are still rising up. With courage and a strong desire, for the reaching out to the Almighty wisdom! We should brace ourselves against the rocks with great confidence. In hope and faith, that the good lord. The creator of all living things! The Holy one of life fulfillment will pull us out of our endeavors.

I press myself in these expressions, for us to come to understand the will of God! There are many of us are going through chronic experiences of tremendous agony. All we should think of, is somewhat are someone; to up lift our hearts spiritually! Have we look around us? We the human generations are having no alternatives to fulfill our conscious desire without divine engagement! As we rise in the morning searching for a resolution. And before goes to rest at night! They are with the same soul searching as human family for divine intervention. It is so amazing when we heard the old saying! That says, time is the Master. Which means the Master work in time; to bring comfort to our humans' hearts. Once we keep on doing the things which is right, to the best of our abilities. We will have happiness, contentment and prosperity; with our lives! The other amazing thing we should see, that God will always come out victorious for us. He always there in our lives. We are the ones who said, I can't do it any longer, or anymore. We should realize the line between God and man, is unconditional not conditional. Don't put God on a belt, I will do this for you God! And you do that for me. There is no deal like that with you and God. He created you and me, so he knows best; for you and me! Not the other way around, his authentic spiritual plans is the best, for our lives. So all the agony and pain, we are facing in every given circumstances. We should bring ourselves in subjection! Of the wisdom and knowledge of God. So his understanding could work for good, in our lives. Let us bring ourselves to find joy, through our pain. Let's find peace in the time of confusion and frustration. Let's us find healing, through the contagiousness of mind pollutions. Let's find dignity and integrity! When our enemies seem as if, they are finding power over the innocent. Just remember that God is standing by. He will not be anywhere otherwise, life is God presence and a gift to mankind!

SPIRITUAL ENERGIES

So who is alive have the presence of God within and around them! Don't worry about the negatives, that plotting against you. Just remember that God is greater, over evil! And if your eggs, is in the basket of the Almighty Creator. You will not be disappointed! Your eggs will not be broken; when your hope and faith, planted on a solid foundation. So that when the storm of life come's, you cannot be shaken down! Because you are spiritually uplifted, spiritually secure! This is a popular saying, show me your company; and I can tell you whom you really are!

SECURITY IN LIFE

For there is no person is going to settle with a company, that he or she don't find favors with.

Which we are not feeling comfortable with, or feeling the positive energy around. Think about the intimate relationship! Once a girl begins to ask the questions, and she is not comfortable with the answers she is getting out! She is not going to stick around, with the guy! But regardless of the conditions, or situations in your lives, come to God. Please realize God will not be going to drop you like a hot potato!

But he's going to teach you intelligence. How to receive the understanding of his wisdom and knowledge! The beauty of which it brings to you. As rewards to your life, that doesn't mean you are not going to face your obstacles! Your struggles of hard times, there can be scary feelings at times. Thinking or wondering, what next bad going to happen. Maybe you thinking, there is trouble a hundred miles! Down the road coming directly for you. So you find yourself in that humbling moments. To pray or to talk to God, asking him to keep you safe. Or to stop these troubles heading towards you. And the great and Mighty One, who is of our lives felt our energy! He connects his mercy, we felt justified within our hearts. In that moment in time, but you must realize that! The Most High God do whatever he please. The Lord can jump right in front of the trouble heading towards you. If he, please to do so. And if he didn't choses to do so! Still know God will always in your favor at all times! But there are times, you my friend has to go through! A little rout in troubles, and I must say. God will be there with you, in every step of the way. For the present of his life in you. As you go along experiencing his confident, and to learn his trust. Which is a part of our legacy, the spiritual walk with him. His holy spirit will teach how to fight our way. When there is trouble, pain and agony. He will embrace us with courage. When we think there is nothing left in you and me as strength! He will show us where to find that little strength to build on. Sometimes it's amazed, how blessings come to your life. Hope and faith is necessary in the journey of life! In that way we will find delight from his benefits. In his company for our lives! Love is always there to warmth our hearts. So we would find peace, joy, loyalty and liberty in happiness. Don't quit on the Lord, and he won't quit on you. And that's security, he's love and light of our world!

And we the human race, are the very essential part of his mystic elements. Through the holy power of God's hope and faith! We put trust in the wisdom, of his great mercy and righteousness towards us! The power of his wisdom water our hearts and soul. His infinite understanding and wisdom, bottled for our lives! By the holiness of his presence.

We are God's earthly angels, who put interest in others wellbeing! We are his soldiers who fight spiritually, for the protection of the Most High creation! In the heavenly place, God's angels bring information to and fro. As life legacy all over the earth. Everything came into existence through his own divine presence! And that the perfection of his Love towards humanity. His greatness is health and healing, to honor the legacy of God. And that's the gifts for every human race to access! The Lord has created and design everything for the benefit of humanity unto his glory. Every facets of God are equally important! In the ability of his own image, such as loyalty. What can we say about the Lord Integrity, and dignity? How pure can it gets, in the sight of his angels and before men? His love is compassion in every given term of consciousness. To pray, is a part of love to have. Unity is also a part of love, loyalty, sincerity, in every given part of his character. Is the ability and image of God's civilized power stand! There is not any future society of this world, or in civilization! Can out run the power of humbleness, which consist in God's Love!

Love is the healing, touch by purity! Give's honor through loyalty! The comfort and the assurance, the light, the spiritual glow, the elevation, the ovation! Love in his qualities, go beyond and back to God. Who is love! Wisdom is to honor the Almighty God; our Creator of all living! Understanding, is what I call {power-standing} is the connector from

God to the human race! And an uplighter for life. It is the tool of our Divine Master, he is gaging and edging the state of our minds! That we may reflect upon his loyalty; and the strength of integrity.

Robert Francis

ENGAGING IMAGES OF CHARACTERS

The wellness of the heart of the human race. Spiritual connection is with the openness, and delightfulness. With confident and courage, it's a life force for the living!

I cannot imagine these four entities, elements or characters. Whatever you may want to label these facets! Which is love, wisdom, knowledge and understanding. These spiritual elements, how could anyone live without these! First I should or may say, the life of our Divine Master. The {Creator, the Almighty}, the {Most High} God. The life of him, is the gift of our legacy! The life of God, could never be in existence; without these spiritual elements? There also couldn't be any wrong and right. Without the whole essence of life, which is the character and life, in God Almighty! These facets are God's holy presence? In the very presence of which we are in existence today. And forever more! So let's come together individually and collectively. To find a way coming to the consciousness of life! By living better, shine better, let's recognize! And to find peace within oneself. Let's unite with that sober voice within your head! He is the voice that calling us to the light of truth, peace and happiness! And place us to where we can come to true contentment? And we should know or acknowledge, there will be barriers and obstacles! In any giving circumstances, as we use confident to gain strength! This is where we can come to understand, it's not shame to face the hard times! It should be a place to fine strength. Throughout your hard times of tribulation! Tell yourself, I will say to the mountain, move! I will fight my way through the valley. And up to the mountain, unto the plain! Say to yourself, I will never stop fight the good fight. Which would cause us to see the light of God promises to life!

Because through the process of fighting, that where you find strength. And that's the kind of strength we are searching for! From whom that is Divine. Courage is when we can monitor yourself! On the journey of life, in a positive sense of life! So that our destiny can result great accomplishment! It is the principles of life that holds us together. Sometimes when we fall, we can remember our roots. Our culture the ways we were brought up by our folks. Our Parents and siblings through the moments of time; things changes!

CHARACTER CHANGES

People changes, the values of life can; as well as the values of life ratings can rise above average and shine! The colors of happiness depending on our minds, to condition our lives! Courage is also what I call confident. And it shouldn't leave the center of your mind. It's a mental and psychological and spiritual settings! A foundation to life, it's the vitality to life. Is that energy that should surface you in high demand of communication! In this world among people. Among others we face issues every day, and that's one of our great demands! Are you ever heard the saying, you have to dance a yard, before you can dance a broad! I think it means to practice principles at home. Families should be connected, from one to the other! It's laying out a brick each moment in time to build a house. Or mansion as a builder! Which we all are, in a different circumstance! We all do different things, but we are building regarding to our future of life! And we always have to use the good things. To direct our lives in the right part! Nobody says we can't make mistakes. And please understand according to the circumstances! Mistake can cause us to feel ashamed. To feel disappointed, even feeling hard to respond, or to take responsibility! A certain mistake, can even make it hard for us to dust off ourselves and try again! Mistakes can cause us to feel anguish and pain. From generation to generation because of traditional principles. We pass on to our future generations! And when I say that, it's because it's in our {DNA} from the time of Adam and Eve mistake in the Garden of Eden! And that was, the receiving the gift of sin. For all generations! Name me, or show me, a living creature. Person or persons upon the face of this Earth! That don't made mistakes, not one mistake but mistakes! But how can we avoid it? By thinking positive, it is to focus on the positive! To tighten up on the better sense of thoughts as our guiding line. Which would be the strength and Loyalty, spiritually of the Almighty! He is the only positive one **in life, and of life. But don't forget this, to reflect your thoughts**! For if mistakes don't made, we cannot be healing upon the circumstances. Which we are hoping for to be heal. It's a spiritual journey for everyone! But within most cases, we have the tendencies to show disrespect to the one. Of whom made the mistake! But that's according to the nature of man. According to the words of the Almighty! Mankind is full of negative behaviors. But we should allow GOD in our lives, through Christ. To teach us forgiveness and positivity, to resist the enemies. By building confident, and to strengthen your loyalty within. Love is always the master of our lives! If we release ourselves from love, the destruction of hate will take over! Time is the makeover, which results our lives. According to our circumstances, it lies with us! When we trust our own life individually! We should also trust in God, because he is life, and the spirit of life! There is no different to trust in your own life; differently from him, for without him we have no life! The common sense of wisdom, just don't comes from your own. But from the true Divine who is of life! He will give his every image to those who seek him.

God, and God alone knows us, when we are in the dust. For I know his forgiveness and mercy and passion. Rides upon us like shining armor, to rise us out of the dust! We shall rise again, to be firm against the negative forces in life! Which is against our will, and to strengthen our subconscious world of life. But as we learn, the true reality to life. Is to fear God and give him thanks! We should bear in mind; God never force us; to do what he asks us to do! For the Lord love is unconditional, and will never change! For any material conditions, but we should keep the loyalty of our heart. To the best of our consistency; so we can walk in the power of love and peace! And that's courage of charity! And that's the perfection we critical of others about? Please consider this, we cannot be perfect through the eyes of our own flesh! But through the eyes of the true divine one. Who is most loyal in his untouchable ways! We are also only perfect by trying to do what is right; within the spiritual eyes of dignity, grace and mercy from the heavenly father! Knowingly we are facing a world of war. But the most effective warfare we are facing today; among the human race, is psychological and spiritual encounter! Which at all times, base our lives on the things which gives us strength; in the positive ways! So we can learn from others, and live for others! The power of life, is about unity. Among humanity, glorifying the Almighty sincerely! Our soul been present by God Most High, upon planet earth. For our benefit came through the image of the God head! For when we think about the concept of life. We can't just think about the flesh and bones in good shapes! As to say looking sexy. Between the physical and the spiritual! Physical always thinking about material things? How to be in power and full control over others and things. Also having money beyond any imaginations! Standing before the world, as one of the greatest Icon. Getting your worldly respect! Yet having no peace in your life. Believed in the wealth than health! Looking upon, as the rich and famous. Spiritual living is about acknowledging the power of nature, through the eyes of the almighty God! Within humbleness, meekness, gentleness and wisdom in mercy! The collectiveness through understanding. The knowledge through sorrows and pain, the strength to rise through the rain. And to with stand troubles like mountains! As the divine power guide us with the shadow of his presence. For his directions, for positive sense.

Many of us don't want to hear the word, {no} or to face disappointments. But most of the time when we heard the word, {no} we feel rejected or mess-up! Dissatisfaction, feeling outlaw, sometimes it will give us the strength. That will trigger our collectiveness of our minds. To restructure our direction and be strong collectively, and individually. We must learn to grow with an open mind in communication towards others! To be understandable with each other's, with the sense of love and kindness! To and fro, with one another. The strength for love and courage, it's not just to keep smiling. But also to embrace others through the tough times, in our lives! We should positively help others to understand circumstances. It's not about winning conversation of others. But apply love and understanding, not for others to feeling bad or upset! Sometimes we are the victims. That doesn't mean we are going too laid down on the ground. And don't want to get back up! Sometimes Selfishness can take over! Or to feeling sorry for one self, will not help the situation to happiness. We are people under the sun, facing Obstacles in life! Engaging to different cultures and Experiences. There are sometimes Circumstances can cost stress and frustrations! But we are the ones to do better, for the benefit of one another. Don't allow others in the mud, for we are of the same! Blood, flesh and bones. We Express our emotions has we know it. We have good and bad emotions, reflecting upon us. We should know how to condition ourselves in relating to others. As we enjoy the vibes, feeling great around others. By feeling the connections from one to the other! Never have you, let go the positive side of strength, which keeps connects us together!

Connecting is a wonderful thing about life! You should make it easy for you, and for others. That's what cause body and life, to be more healthy! So happiness can spread more abundantly. For the wellness of the whole human race! Love give energy like the sun by day. Without love there is no peace or contentment. No joy or happiness, no Grace or mercy, no togetherness in unity. Patience, hope, faith in each other's! Love have the roots in all of these character! Love is the corner stone to lean on.

MIND AND SOUL INSPIRATIONS

Our hearts and soul can be amend; through spiritual attention! Where are we today with each other's, within ourselves? Are we feeling the pure touch of emotions? No corrupt thoughts against your brothers and sisters! Love is the fruit that nourishes our hearts and body, Mind and soul! Love always pure to us; on a higher ground. It is his Grace that should reflects us, of what one can see within us as a person! Life is a beautiful gift, that naturally glow, its pure natural beauty. Nature is beyond limits, entering in all forms, shapes and sizes uniquely. And should be free, but how could we be when we have a certain kind of boundaries, and security!

LIMITATIONS

The innocents are facing penalties, and injustice is prevailing! Anger spread the results of someone death. Revenge step in and made it more dread? What happening to the world of society, in? the Negative sides of the human race. We keep busted because of the wrong things we did! We are broken down; we are broken up. Light don't shine in light, so we can close our eyes and walk! If it does so, by making the lights becomes brighter. And I'm talking the spiritual and moral standard, of the human race, or mankind! The light shines through darkness, so that one can see each step making! As we balance ourselves through conscious decisions. Sometimes between the rock and hard places! Or when our back against the wall, we have to come up with the most honest decision, getting out of situations. There is a saying that said. He that walked with the wise, shall be wise! But he that walk with the fools, shall be more foolish. Because the darkness can't shine through the light, but the light through darkness! Only the heart knows his bitterness. For the crown of the wise, is their loyalty and integrity! But the foolishness of fools, is their folly. You can't do the wrong and get right. Neither should you do the right. And it results you wrong! Under the spiritual code in life. But with the prideful and prejudice. They accused and abused and mist-used. Because the dark is against the light. And hate is against Love, bad is against good! The innocent inherits injustice, while the mischievous enjoy freedom! And the hungry dies for wants. Where did the world turn upside down! When love and justice is still here. We are allowing ourselves to be fools. And to be deceived by the negative forces of our minds! Switchon your light so you can see. Where you are going, it's a long journey ahead of you! So make sure you keep your head up. Open your heart for love to come in. for the world shines against the spiritual side of life! So therefore we in a society world of controversy, contradictions, with great convictions in their own ties, or believed! We should use Love and courage, to stick together as human race. When we understand love to a level. We will grow with conviction to ourselves and for others. Courage brings out the determination through love for others! Love is the back bone and corner stone of one's life! Without love, we cannot dwell on the positive. To allow courage to prove its way for prosperity! We the human race, should move away the grudge, from our minds and hearts. And allow the power of wisdom in, from love! To bring more strength to our happiness in our lives! We are standing on a ground that should determine our destiny. We should use love and courage, learning the power of forgiveness. How to forgive one another, so we can free ourselves, from vengeance and revenge. From one, or to the others.

One should ask for forgiveness; to settle the core of the wrongs we did. We will always have our conscience barking out within us! To lay out the good settings, and make adjustment against the wrong things we did. We know blessings comes from a pure heart. When we practice to be loyal to ourselves, and to others! And the spirit of understanding, as to say! That wisdom can lead us to peace, prosperity and contentment to our soul. When we find the tools to enjoy the journey of life. We will broaden our levity, and grow strong in the sight and power of Love. As we represent our lives! For the sun, moon and stars hangs over us. To remind us of the mystic power that represent our lives. As we uphold our hopes and dreams! With the knowledge says, no man is an island, no one stands alone! For a merry heart is medicine to the soul. And the words of a man's mouth are as deep water. And as the spring of wisdom! Like a flowing brook. We are all on planet Earth. Looking out for each other's wellbeing! We are mystically connected through the powers of the Most High God. Through his positive attributes such as. Peace, love and loyalty within the courage of the minds! The mind is a home that accommodate the positive, and the negative. As a result of the negative! We inheriting confusion, fuss and fighting, wars and crimes.

Hatred, grudge, sabotaging, brutalization and Abuse. Which leads to agony, starvation and Emotional and physical pain. So on and so forth!

The only way to bring back prosperity. Is to capture the sense of Love and Courage. So we can think positively, by feeling the peace and

Love and Courage

trusting within ourselves. Individually and collectively! Then we can find the strength of dignity and integrity supplementing, the human Soul. As human race grasp on more consciousness, of our wellness. As we faithfully hold our grounds, with hope never ending! Through the power and the will of the Almighty. The Most High One, who created the heaven and the earth. And all living things that has been on this earth and above! We all are authentically in the present of his mystifying power. Fighting through struggles, and trying to do what is right! But sometimes as we know, the wrong gets a strong hold of us! In a very nasty way, but by holding your head above; towards his careful guidance. Listening to his soft still voice, as to what I would call your conscience. Which we have ignored millions of times. And his voice of your conscience, is there to speak again. And over again with a spirit of full control and serenity! It's like with no fear; you have a divine entity connection! You can claim anytime to wipe away transgression! As to which I could say, we are to bring our mind back to reality and peace. The power of forgiveness as came to your rescue, and settle the score with Love from above! Nothing can stop a good man. Please, let me say it another way! There are no evil forces can stop the goodness in someone. Because you see, the power of goodness transform himself! In the shape of flesh and bones, that's where love and goodness dwell. And I say {himself} he is a Character. So don't be afraid to call on the true divine power. Because you think you done the worst of the worst. He is not going to turn his back on you! Once you say you want to talk with him. It's because you thinking of some changes, guess what. We all need a second chances, forgiveness has the power, with Love!

My grandma used to say, you do well you do yourself! And if you do badly, you do it to yourself. Because whatsoever a man sow. that shall he reap, as to say, what goes around, comes right back to you as a result! We should know how to escape these bad turns in life. It's best sincerely to ask for forgiveness! To release yourself from the bad ties; that give your freedom. With the power of forgiveness! This strength of serenity, {forgiveness} have no colors. Only to bring your mind in subjection to humbleness. And you will see the power of humility transcend from your heart and soul. And your mind becomes burden- less without pain! But to refill us with the strength of joy. Knowingly that you are completely fill with the power and strength! Of the free spirit which surrounds you.

Which gravitating your soul! Love is not cheap, neither the spirit of God. His blood run through our veins, he's the creator of every single planet in existence! How much more bigly, you want him to get for you. Have you not seeing enough realities! That could draw you to his conviction. There is no one can have approved of his or her self, in any existing planets! That can reach beyond the knowledge of the Most High God! His timeless character and his unspeakable glory and joy, is fathomless to all generations! In present and the future. Everything that he handed over to us, is freely given! And it's of him, or we are the shadow of him, through his Love, mercy and grace! In full in the abundant, we are not limited to his searching!

By giving yourselves to the light of his consciousness. Is to bring ourselves under subjection to his truth! Or under the true meaning of life. That's beyond your human purpose of living! Your human purpose, is different from God purpose. But has we surrender our hearts and minds. In union and unity to the powers of the Most High! Who is so ever living, and so ever sure? And so faithful, he is the beginning and the everlasting! No human race can out run his life. It's not an easy road to tread to our destiny! But it's very good finding time to enjoying the journey. It's the purpose of life, more well and meaningful, in the light of prosperity! And that's a pure energy to feel through your heart and soul. When we feel connecting with the positivity of life! We should feel like a young plant by the water brook.

Love and Courage

Beauty lives within confidence, as a result of bringing peace to the mind for happiness to reign. And love is the power which keep us satisfied, so that unity can keep us together!

STRENGTH OF LIGHT

Absorbing the richness from the soil as a blessing to our spiritual growth! Times after times, we will learn stage by stage. We should learn how to value, and accept the blessings of what life achievements are. Has we going the distance of our circumstances. Bottling our way against the negatives! Nothing else can comfort or to fulfill our soul than with a positive mind! We use the positive, to close in the gapes of the negatives! And let love fight with all our might and energy of the positive, to the road of victory. Try your very best, not to allow your mind to engage to the negative energy. It is hard when everything is up in our face, making headline to deceive your mind! Don't let go the courage and strength of the positive. There is a reward behind the curtains. We just got to keep trying, and keep stepping closer to the truth! With honor and integrity. The steps are not easy, but through the grace of his infinite power. Who is the exceedingly boundless One! We the human race of this world, we are to look within ourselves. For the meaning of our feature, is towards the purpose of our lives! We also have to engage our minds with good intensions for self, and for others! We should all bring good imagination to reality. Therefore, we should be very concern about our destiny! Life is so fragile, everything is here just for a while? Take the time to know someone. Let the power of love begins! Let love be your friend, once it begins there will be no end! Love is life shinning beauty, its character that always caring, always sharing! Love is the light that always shining through. The heart allowing the mind to connects to the soul. Breaking down all particles into the positive links, of life journey! We should try to humble ourselves to every given situation. Connects with our emotions of the positive. I will be the first to admit that it is not an easy task. But I know that through the power; and the will of our Creator. All things are possible through the eyes of his divine love. We would be like fools, when we keep hurting someone! And it causes also, hurting ourselves! And we would also be like fools, when we are revenging someone. We also hurt ourselves when hurt others. Because deep within ourselves, we know it's wrong! Regardless of the negativities may shapes our way. We will always know wrong from right! The very meaning of life, we should take to consideration; just for the beauty of communication. So we can always secure the values of our lives security! The strength which we maintain over the years, as a proper training in all of these facets! Character brings out our potential as civilized people, or civilized families! Wisdom, understanding and knowledge, we should try look within these facets! So we can determine where we are in each image of approach! As we anchor ourselves in the way love wants us to be. We will foresee behind and beyond the curtains of life. How could we think that love will disappoint us? In any form or shape of life destination, or along life journey! The beauty and the essence of living, is to appreciate life! Appreciation is the caring, sharing. The mercy and the forgiveness, these are some of the ingredients. Or character building which grows with life prosperities! Blessings comes from the divine infinite One. Who holds us in the directions, has he created us to be. But his unconditional and infinite Love sees us; through the eyes of his mercy, grace and forgiveness! Has we jump short, in our doings. But regardless of how many times we bring ourselves to our short coming. We know strongly on what ground we are anchored. Within the contentment of our lives! The promises which has made known of his righteousness. It is because of the foundation; which love came from! Within the existence of life, Love made us valuable through his grace and mercy! By the image of whom is the center of these characters. For the image of God is the image of man, through the life of his holy spirit! The almighty God breathe into every flesh and bones. But unto mankind, God imputed his wisdom. Which is God spiritual presence. Our bodies he created, is the temple of where his holy spirit dwells! Which we became living soul, by his majesty. Bearing the awesomeness of his wisdom understanding and knowledge! Is the whole divine revelation that should enlighten the whole image of God in men! But because of the catastrophe taken place in the Garden of Eden! Speaking of our short coming. Our father's Love has spread through the eyes of his forgiveness! So we can find hope in faith! To received his mercy. We are naturally growing divinely, seeing the light from the dark! As the dark hold us down, in contempt against the right! The beauty of love opens to everyone. To feel to see, and to understand, love separates us from the negative of darkness! For every man's life have a value to be judge by their integrity. Observance, love is of God. Love in is purity, as called out through faith in wisdom. By the power of knowledge and understanding!

All these are of the same divine character, as a reflection before the infinite mirror of the Most High. The Almighty God who stand, in the awesomeness of his glory. We are of his Master piece of his creation.

LEGACY TO YOU

His handmade, his image, it's the characteristics of life beauty! The holiness of his divine touch. Jehovah God is love, and love is the very touch of his righteousness. The very gift of man's life, is the very beauty in the experiences; which brings happiness! The very nature, that distribute the spiritual experiences of happiness. Is a blessing to generations after generations! We have to connect as generations. Has human, as people, to spread the river of loyalty to each other's. Has much as we can, knowing in reality we are not perfect. But by wearing the crown of unity, will cause us to be content. In mind and spirit with one another! We should be on our diligence in awareness of the dark forces. The master of deception, send out his agents. To break down the defense of the poor and needy! So we can be trample under feet. As in connection and collaboration with the system world of society. The rich are getting greedy; it doesn't matter what it takes. To climb on the shoulders of others, by getting what they need. In terms of keeping others down. Has we the poor experiencing the aches and pain! The feelings of others are of no values to the world of society. The poor and needy is affected, by such level and stages, of their struggles! Every members of political leaders. Thinking they are doing their best, in every stage or stages! Even though their mind is of folly tricks. The bottom line, the political system of the world societies. Is not bringing love to the neighbor, or the neighborhood! But in the eyes of justice, according to political system. Their love is of wars, pain and agony towards the human race. It's became catastrophe beyond the human conditions. Of which they cannot hold the pain any longer! The human race families and friends, became frustrated. Turning on each other's like wild beast. All manner of evil is taken place under the sun! Rape, killing, stealing and separation with love ones. With parents and children, families against families! Nations against nations breaking down kingdom! Because we are locking of his infinite wisdom! Knowledge and understanding of the divine power of creation. If we as people who with the power, to respect the doings of what God did. For this creation, we would protect our environment. And not to destroy it, or to destroying ourselves! When the nations locking of wisdom, the people perishes. But if we should link in with the power of unity. All of creation will acknowledge how valuable love is to us collectively! And this what the pure divine is portraying unto us the human race!

The pure endless Love, which stand in his own category. Spotless, untouchable with great mercy and forgiveness! Authentically reaching out from the heart of divinity. Only if we could be sustaining with courage. To have an open heart, mind and soul! Never-the-less we could be strengthening, from one to the other! Through the will of his divine present. We will all inherited our legacy which as provide for us, as human race. Love and courage as we know, by the will of his infinite wisdom. Should have an impact on our lives, the way we are living! Our character of integrity through the almighty will. Should find ways, determining how we are living! Our blessings come from above, through an everlasting kingdom power!

We should not grudge or hate each other's. If and when we do so, envying what others have! We are only targeting ourselves! Taken away our own blessings. Because with the hate within our hearts. We will be punishing by God, through the hands of men. And there will be no greater punishment, than when we are punishing by the almighty God! Prosperity given to us when we fellow the love rules. Because there is no greater way to find communication! Than through Love, when you have love unconditionally in your soul! You set upon a throne, which the divine majesty has given to you. As an inheritance, Love and courage is a spiritual remedy! For these powers came from above. To the heart, soul and mind, these are the roots of life! And a healing to the nations.

Love help us to redefine our lives. When our lives get crooked, when we face the struggling through the dark. When agony and pain shapes the results to our lives. When the mountains get higher, and the rivers rises up! And we can't cross to the other side. Courage is in the bosom of

Love and Courage

Love. Will takes us anywhere to a safe place! By the hands of the Most High God! Regardless of what we may be going through. We should be strong in our minds. Don't run away from what you going through. It will only face you another day. Or it will even become harder for you, because you are not thinking of resolution. But only to run! Or only to be afraid of what may happen. We are only calling down worst situation on ourselves! Facing circumstances, is to focus on the positive side. Be a real revolutionary and call out to Love and courage. From the power of the Most High, the holy true divine power of creation! The giver of life, and solver through the time of our bumpy road in Life! When the test of faith comes, and hope as lost its shadow! Love has a way to trigger courage through wisdom. Understanding will inform hope, to the invitation in faith! Has we struggles with our circumstances. The spirit of the father will enlighten our strength with his knowledge! Remember there is so much experiences in life to bump into! But we must be strong in courage with Love. The hills and valleys, the high mountains. As rough as it may get in our lives! Has we facing the different stages in life. Just remember love and courage, have a great part to play. On the positive side of our lives! Please allow the journey of our lives to be excited, enjoyable! In that divine direction, and there will be no obstacles or barriers. Which will stand before you, that can't be challenge, or to be remove! Because every man can do all things, through the infinite power! Who give us strength throughout our lives? God in his divine authentic present, already removes our burden! But we have to have confident in his trust, strongly in our mind! Then the next step is to take actions, as the good lord leads the way! And we will see the reality as a result! Everything have set in place, by the true divine one. Action verse reaction, or as to say that. Every action gives an equal reaction. Staging on the level or the kind of life we are living! Or the type of environment we choose to be into! Life is a gift, which resulting our legacy! Has we nourished our minds in the positive ways.

Keep this one thing in mind, we don't have to have a lots of material things! In our position, and millions of dollars to be rich. It is the qualities which we show in our lives! Made us divinely rich, because material riches having no substances! Comparing to divine riches. Because divine riches work on our emotions. From our hearts, soul and minds, through the agony and pain!

Robert Francis

AGONY WITH INTEGRITY

A m talking about struggling, the obstacles you and I face. Will strengthen our image and integrity! So don't matter how hard you are shaken down. There is a sense of pride that will never be touch!

Are shaken, because we understand the test. Which can bring us down between the cliffs of rocks through tribulations! We face or been through, we stand firm by revolutionizing our mind facing the positive! Through the hard core hungriness and emotional walls, sleeping on the streets. The test we face, it's like processing clay through the fire. As the clay remains cure! So is our loyalty remains us pure which reflects unto us. It is big core for us through the divine present! We can show the glory and strength as a results of our salvation. Has one feel the energy from the humbleness of others they experience! We all have qualities in unification, coming from love! In most cases material riches cannot and will not! Go through the test, which divine strength as gone through and endure! Because all who's minds are materialistic. Have no strength for divine endurance!

I am giving a hands out to all the people of this world! Both small and great, the rich and the poor, the weak and the strong! The envious and the kindhearted, open your window of your mind! And move away the curtains of grudge, penalization. From among us as a nation and family, of this wonderful world! It's time to redefine our lives, or to come to redemption! Individually and collectively as a people of the human race. Ask yourselves this question, how we could fine prosperity without uniting with each other's! Let's start within from our own hearts. At home, in the office, in the conference room. Before you take up the gun, to go and hunt your own humankind down! Think about unity of oneself and forgiveness. There is a line between good and evil. I know you know what's the consequences are? From either side, so be patient with yourself. To make the decision right, and remember that love's anchors it all! We also should acknowledge that we are not in a perfect world. But trying our best is all we can do. We should have love to see the safety and prosperity of each other's. We are like chain to its links, looking out in respect for one another! In the same breath of doing well to others. Is the same as doing well to yourself! Just likewise if you are doing the bad. The greatest writer says, whatsoever a man sowed that shall he reap. You can't wrong and get right, neither can you right. And get wrong, in the divine and infinite present. For there is no man that is greater than his conscience! Because that's where the Almighty One, is presence in your soul! But he will not force you. To take control of the positive! It is powerfully natural for a man in contentment. To do what is right in the sight of love! And the lines of the positive, is of what brings peace. From his divine grace, and unto happiness. Loyalty, prosperity, courage, dignity and integrity! When you are not force to the right. By doing this naturally on your own! Through the eyes of wisdom, knowledge and understanding. You are far more in control spiritually. With great contentment, confident and sustainable amount of hope. In faith of doing things, has we learn through experiences! That patient is one of the key note in life.

The true light of love shines in billions of ways. Through the circumstances of which our ways of living exist! Every given situation is equal to its resolution, through everlasting love! On the other side of nature. We mankind have no patience for others. The innocent lost their lives, because of the dark side of human nature! We throw others in the mud. We indulge to see others, causing others pain and agony! It's like the dark, became light. And hate became love, and destruction became paradise. And weapons of mass destruction became a safety rod for the rebellious, of the human race! While the innocent living in insecurity throughout their lives! For this pace of which the rebellions of wars are going! Consider twenty more years from now. What a great amount of catastrophes this world will be experiencing! There will be no one hardly to be trusted. You and I will never know who will be our enemies, from your friends! We will be laughing with each other's, and still nervous with one another! In this conditions of our future. How are we going to find true happiness and prosperity? We should now put way our urgency of pride. And icon ship and fame, let's stop playing the losing game. Which causing the precious lives of love ones, and family! Look deep within, and listen to your conscience. Through the eyes of wisdom, the father of creation! In his spiritual present he's observing our unwilling quality. Has we turn our back to his graceful qualities. Living in the age without self-control, is tampering our own soul. Ask yourself these questions, when and where. And how can we get out of these trap! This is a psychological and mental enslavement. We are fooling ourselves, as human race!

Love and Courage

We can relax our mind with conscious music, which reflects the strength of our lives...

ABILITIES OF CONFIDENCE

We are lacking the trueness of our passion, in accordance with communication! From one to the other, we therefore living like enemies as people and nations! We at this point, where life don't seem to have much spiritual values. It's like we became hunters for human lives. We are not thinking, or to understand the basis facts of humanity! When we hurt others, taking their lives, or causing pain. We are not making solution in any situation! Mankind is making situations gets worst, with our lives involves!

Now is the time more than ever, to show unconditionally the Love! Than to show love with conditions. By tying something to the love you are showing to someone. You remember the greatest writer says. It's better to give than to receive. And to love your neighbor, just the way as you love yourself! Just think of it this way. Once a man love himself in the true sense. He is spiritually connected with that unconditional love; he found treating himself with! You will show it to others like wise. For we know love is the Master of life! We have the brains, minds and great potential in knowledge. To know why we are receiving the blessings of peace and prosperity! Is therefore when we are authentically giving; we don't have to worry about receiving. For if giving is a blessing, then receiving is rewarding! Which is a blessing also! Life have a great sense of values in prosperity. Life is to be free, through the divine sense of wisdom, knowledge with understanding!

I want to invite you to a little information here. Says the little that a righteous man has. Is better than the riches of disloyalty! Love and courage and endurance is strength. Is our refuge in the present? time of trouble! Love reign and courage explain footsteps in reality! When love call your name. And courage prints your name on your heart! Would you turn your back against the will of God purpose, for your life? As a chance to walk between the stars; or to be touch by the galaxies! Would you see the light and allow yourself, to be overcome by the dark? It would be like mocking yourself foolishly; against righteousness! Or against the wisdom of the Master! Could it be your life stepping into the paradise of wickedness? Which could allow the purpose of your life, becoming meaningless! Stand firm as a soldier of consciousness. Against delusion, temptations and frustration! Gideon spiritual war fare, we should stand and state our values in lives! What is our concern that make us strong to the core? Is the passion in knowledge, courage, wisdom and understanding; made us find our ways for survival? Through these merciless times of the human crises! We cannot keep living, in fool's paradise. We have to stand up and fight with courage. With a higher spiritual volume for our lives! We need the integrity and charity to show the world that without Love; there wouldn't be any creation! This creation existence is through the power of love! And that's the same love cause us to be connected has humanity! So therefore we should build our life foundation with love. Because the courage we show to ourselves. And to others, it's a sense of values upon our integrity! Life is a very beautiful facets. I said this more than twice. That we are not in a perfect world! But we can't allow ourselves to be deceive by others! Or to deceived others. It is right in the conscience of nature, that says! Don't do to others, the things you don't like them do unto you! It would be unfair to do others wrong. And don't expect the result of wrong to come back to you! Remember it already lay out in the tread mark of our nature. Action verses reaction, think about this! If this world in total, should go down in destruction? Where would be the grace of love? The grace is a spiritual energy that heals our heart and free our equality, has humanity! It's an unspeakable energy that pass on to nature. Bottom line, grace is of love, the present of the Almighty! With all the destruction that this world is into. Life will never totally erase from mankind! Because God is still in control, over the universe. Why this world is going through destruction; because we the generation is drifting away, from grace and love! So can we see how important the purpose of life; needs the grace of God's love? Love is strength, love is freedom, courage, loyalty, peace and unity! And all the rest follows.

We made it appeared in the eyes of misunderstanding. In relationship with the Almighty Father. Has if he owes us something like obligation! Throughout our circumstances, or situations! Let me turn on a question to you gracefully! If the sun was to stop shine for a year. Have you known the purpose of the sunshine? What would that do for us? Or for the living things. The light of the sun gives us energy. And the rest of the living things. You don't have to imagine what would happen to our lives! If the sun stops shines for one year. Actually you know what could happen. We would have lost great amount of energy! No supplements could give us entirely what the sunshine have in store for us! Most of us would be mentally stress out. And there is nothing, we have a human race, could do about it! When the power of nature takes its course; as the world say, Mother Nature. We should believe that is the hands of the Almighty! Who is so everlasting, so ever living, and so ever faithful; so ever sure, the divine master of the universe. Just think about the tornado and the storm! We knew it was coming, and there is no human being, couldn't stop any of these disaster, for the purpose of saving other's lives! Because the way we are so inhuman against one another; they are not recognizing the true grace of the divine power! Life need gentleness to inhabit the blessings, as a result of our lives. There is strength we must share positively amongst ourselves; has mankind. So throughout all our lives, we can inherit the powers of prosperity! Love as the answers to every given circumstances. And a result to very human being on this planet earth. Are we ready to embrace righteousness? Through love in the eyes of his divine presence! And be satisfied step by step, with the little we received each day! Which would give us strength every moment. To jump over the hurdles, to climb over mountains. And to make giant steps through the valleys of our lives! The journey of life will never end, until the strength of our body give in. but we all should know our steps and boundaries. While we keep on broken down walls and barriers, in our lives! Just remember that love always be the door to the master! Who we should give control over our heart and soul. Nothing greater, when we can allow gentleness through the eyes of love, to take over!

Love shines positively, never put you down. Love raise you up, and will not allow you to fall to the ground! The sustaining power of love will never drain your battery. But motivate the substance of your light to shine brighter! What can we do together, to embrace the Qualities of life! In our beautiful environment. We should rise up together and fight to free the bondage. And cause for good qualities towards the minds of the whole human race! This world should result us more on a positive level. And to delete the grudge from our lives, through the eyes of Love. The purest energy to purify the earth. We have the freedom to breathe the fresh air as people! Without the cause of material position. This is the gift we should loyally embrace. For the benefit of happiness and prosperities. No man is an island, no one stands alone! Let us embrace our humanity through the gift of life! What more can we ask of within the destiny of our lives. When we swipe away the bad memories from within our lives! By the courage, love and forgiveness we are processing from within.

LEGACY OF THE DIVINE

Through the giving of the divine, the corner stone of our life destiny!

Every man in his existence of life, has given an opportunity in the sight of freedom! But because of the inhuman nature of our negativity; of all the given societies around the globe, resulting the insecurities, causing agony and pain. Crimes and delusions massively! All over the world sadness and stress, take over happiness. Insecurity take over security! Contentment and peace is gone out of sight, and out of minds. We have people cannot be aware of the place where we stand. We lost the glow of our spirit positively, and our living became intensely. Our roots and cultures buried under our feet! We are standing on the sand which keep sinking; because we made bargain against the rock of our foundations! We are losing in our angry state of mind, while our grievances pushing us deeper in the mud. How can we have human comes to the truth, or realities! We are going deeper into destruction. The innocent is letting go from their integrities. They can't feel the strength of grips holding on anymore! To the source of knowledge, wisdom and understanding! When are we going to let go the materiality of insecurities? And to find positivity of our lives. I will hope to see the days, when the morning sun rises. As a new changes of generations, to a happier world. A satisfying people where we stand up for our responsibilities! By seeing the fruits and other foods becomes plentiful. As a blessing, and animals heals to mankind command. And will be no drought or starvations! The earth will sustain with water from the rain. And as we grow and spread with love through his Divine presence. The poor and weak will be experiencing something wonderful in this life era! So once more we can see the beauty, of heaven and earth. While we step by step escape the fool's paradise!

Communications keep a civilized world connected. But the fools and ignorant always blame the innocent, for their dirty cause. Serenity will not show its values; until man or person accept the truth has his closest friend. Deep inside we think we are wise; only because sometimes we tried to out run our neighbors knowledge! Thinking that we are wiser. Can you feel the ignorance traveling through the air? Blowing in our faces, it's your conscience, which you can't resist! To you, your pride of deceptions; revealing to you, a delusional state of mind! Which sometimes many of us cannot resist! Even when the truth knocks us in the face, our pride just can't accept defeat! This is where we are, individually and collectively, burn by evil prompt! It's so hard for families to reunite, because of the ignorant side of this society embraces pride! Which fight against the pure natural strength of forgiveness! And also throw the power of intelligence out through the door. Just think about this for a while; in any given circumstances, when a person turns their back on forgiveness! They turn their back on the progression of their own life! Even though in some situation or circumstances, forgiveness is very hard to do! But we should also know that, the strength of life; is part of what generates us from the source of forgiveness, through love!

We have to redefine ourselves, within the state of our minds! To revalue oneself, by seeing how relatively important, we are in this cosmic world! We are no more important, or lesser important than each other's! We are no more perfect, or lesser perfect than each other's! Think about it for a while. Even though we may not mess-up the same way as others does! We should remember that it is according to the circumstances. When we mess-up in our lives. How wrong could that wrong be? To the description of the wrong! You still resulting from your wrong actions. When comes on the other side of life. Living right, resulting your happiness! But how much more happiness; you could be enjoying living right in your material world? Different from the person who is rich with integrity, poor materially, but accept the level of Qualities. He or she is living their lives; because remember, rightful living brings happiness! Once you accept the stage of your qualities, of rightful living! You should be happy, if you say you are not happy. It is because you are retracting the conditions of your living! And you cannot come to accept the terms or circumstances, of your life style! For example, if we have a bad weather in the summer season. Where everything should be looking green and healthy. But there is gusty wind and no rain, and there is sunshine of great heat. That will describe to be the bad weather. I doubt it, that we may have a healthy summer season! That's the way it's so important with forgiveness in our civilized world. For what should be good, becomes bad, forgiveness is like spring time, and summer time! When the rain falls, and the sun comes out; with the calmness of the wind that blows across the prairies! So is love and courage changes the atmosphere of our lives.

What we should be fighting for, or standing up for? When we are connecting with each other's. In this world as a human race, life was always and is always the important factor. With the tools of knowledge, wisdom and understanding; is to shape up life in the positive directions! Within the extent of this civilized world, planet earth needs to survive through our positive ways from our conscious mind. We are existing every day on planet earth for a reason and a purpose! When we are born has babies growing up. And being nurtured by family until we grown up to maturity. Then we take on responsibilities by the choice we made and makes! These are some of the purposes, in our lives. Along with the kind of tools we used in some of the circumstances, in life! We should understand our purposes and responsibilities. To make it work for our prosperities. Throughout our communications and connections in our relationships. Positive relationship is a blessing for us has human being. Love, courage, peace and integrity along with faith and hope to navigate, our journey in life! The power and the fulfillment is within us, and from us! Through the strength of these tools we are using. To connect our journey to our destiny?

The quality of life has all the attributes to bring us, to the light and truth! As we develop a conscious mind connecting with our environment. We not aware sometimes of our unknown experiences!

How hard can it be when it comes! It can be the storm of our lives. Blow us away off our feet, leaving us with no standing ground! So to be with the strength, we have to understand the level. The magnitude of our hard core tough times experiences; we went through! And has you may be going through now. In this case you connect the pass and present! To find the resolution, we have to seek out love with courage. by putting on our armor to protect ourselves, from the dark age of destruction! As we keep going on surviving throughout our experiences we face each moment! So we armor up like a man of war. By putting on the helmet, for the readiness of mind! The shield of faith for the confident to fight through whatever the circumstances maybe! Peace, is when others throw words at you enviously. Allow the peace of the Almighty to transcend all understanding to overcome evil! Then put on the breastplate to safeguard your heart from the spear and sword! When it comes at you. Consider this, we are fighting against the wrong things. Even though we can't be perfect all through our lives! But we still have to put up that fight against evil. To declare your good character in the eyes of love and courage. Wear the belt of truth, so you can stand in the presence of loyalty. Stand up with the sword of justice, harmony! Your victory which you have accomplish on the road of life journey, to your destiny! Here I present to all human race. To put away the hate and grudge, and fight with love collectively, as one nation! Because on this planet earth, we can make this world a better place to be!

Robert Francis

RIGHTFUL GROUND

We are the source of each other's, so let's come together. To this one common Gold. Please beware of the truth! We are connected has a people, as a race, as a nation, and as humanity! Why it is so hard to admit to the strength of understanding. Why we fight so hard sometimes; and to ignore what is right; For the benefit of our lives? For the things that we should do, we do not! And the things we should not do, that's what we do in a very often way. We fight against our conscience just to revenge others. And even though we think we are satisfied, when we respond harshly to others! I tell you, you are not satisfied. Because that little voice inside your head who is Mr. Conscience. Speaking so softly letting you know it's not right! Life is a pure gift from above, without charge for any material position! But only to treat life with the best of your ability! With the help from above. And there are ways to receive that help! Is to find that courage to be humble. It's like entering through a gate to see Mr. Humbleness! But as you get closer to the gate to rest your hands on it. You knew if pushing that gate, there will be some current would be shacking you. With a voice saying don't open that gate! You are not allowing to enter. But it's all leave to you, of understand what humbleness means to you! What is the benefits for your life, connecting with the strength of humbleness? You have to find the courage, strength and determination to push harder!

On the gate of Mr. Humbleness, even to find a way to connects in communication! By letting go of oneself, with an open mind to see the difference! Communication is a great deal of connections towards the human race. Communication is to keep connecting with the understanding! Throughout the circumstances which is in hand. Is not about who is right or wrong, it's about connecting with the understanding, within the situations! Dealing with so many. Therefore, person can respond to each other's. With satisfaction of the spirit within! That's a great deal of transcending power to the people or person.

Consciously and positively knowing your right. Which is a part of your freedom, once you aware of your rights!

SPIRITUAL BENEFICIARY

You should not worry, because your integrity should keep your rights. Deep inside of you there is a sense of pride; which no one can take away! They only can take the privileges away from you! That doesn't mean that the takers have your rights; because they take away the privileges! No, you still have your rights! The takers do the wrongs, by taking away your privileges. The access or the chances to the freedom, to enjoy your rights! And also consider this, the power is still with the rights of yours! Through the keeping up of your integrity. That sustaining strength which motivates you characteristically. But please be aware sometimes, you can lose your rights! Which is your own freedom in circumstances or situations! Which you may act out on negatively. So in return you becomes the wrong doer. As a result, you struck with sadness and regrets. This is one of the reasons why you have to be InTouch with communications! Once you are connecting with understanding, your rights are seal within you. And your integrity with more sustaining strength. Life is freedom. And that's where the eyes of knowledge, wisdom and understanding should be! To the underlining of the situation, or as to say. (Eyes it up, and size it up)! By doing so positively. The human race will able to rise to the Heights of intelligence! On the arising of this civilized world; as a result, to happiness and prosperity. There will be peace replenish you, gracefully!

There is another way to think positively on the evidences of life, which the words bear the burdens to excite our heart and soul! Will the truth of life, lighten our way? When we think that maybe, there is no way through our tough times in our lives? And please take note of this, it's always someone to bring us words of great comfort! Which cease moments

Robert Francis

If we put away our differences, and learn to trust within ourselves as people and as a person we will always find it within our heart to forgive others…

of agony and pain. Never to worry, when you are thinking and living positively. There will always good reward to your life as a result! As if you are touching by an angel hand. Which to say, if you always allow your spirit; connecting with the conscious side of life. Trusting in the positive of life, into what the words bears the burden! To transcend to your minds, soul and heart. By hearing the voice of your conscience, refreshing your thoughts! Like the arising morning breeze. Keeping you on a stands of enthusiasm. Which of the morning sun? And as freshness of the will take away your frustrations and confusion! By bringing you to a place, as if you just enter into a new world! With such a confidence; that you will never go back to where were. But to move forward to a shining beauty, of which life attain and contain! To the heights of its greatness. As we keep looking upward asking ourselves the question. How anyone could rise to this occasion of this magnitude; of uplifting stage by themselves? Individually it would be impossible, because we are attach and connects to each other's. You should not say you don't know where you are! Or don't know where you from, on the face of this planet earth. We are the human race, and the source of life will not separate us! For any reason at all, we were created this way. To keep connecting, and that's what love and courage is all about; never to end! Love is the energy which send off the flares of the light! For everyone to see (Love) his beauty in action. Courage is to stand with love, as a strength of integrity! To be sustain with continuation, courage is a company of love and life style! It's an element that causing love to shine limitless! Love mystified the understanding to life. As a result, that wisdom and knowledge be a companionship! With a seal of promises, that no negative force will break their union! That the power of love.

Selfishness is enmity against forgiveness. And forgiveness is at the border line giving strength to the courageous. Of who have the vision and vitality; to share with those who have the discerning energy? To resist the negatives against the force of selfishness! But for those who came half way on the journey. And feeling very weary, falling out of divine and mental energy. Think of the obstacles in mind and thoughts. Holding back the progress of their spiritual state of concept! While forgiveness stand firm at the gate calling out a loud to you. Saying I will find a little more step; of inviting you closer to the Experiences, of strength and courage have to offer you! There is love through the power of forgiveness. The confidence that you should be wearing! It would be an armor against selfishness. By taken the time to know someone with an open mind. Processing yourself for the trueness of life. The divine love we received for ourselves; is the same love we will be showing to others? Just remember at all times, to be on your Q's; of awareness! Of what selfishness can do to destroy your life! Be against the negative force of darkness. And where there is pride, there is negative forces. And the presentation of pride, can appeared so genuine! So here I submit my advice to you. Plant your feet on solid ground! Which is to say, allow your heart, soul and minds. In the awareness to think positively, with the best of your ability!

I will also say this to you with courage. And to the encouragement, that love covers all fears and impurity! And we have to challenge ourselves, with the best of our ability. To see the results of what love can do for our lives. I describe love as a character, which speak deep inside our minds. Love is good, and good is over evil! I hope you understand what I'm saying. And where I'm going with this statement. That every person should have equality. To every giving terms, and every situation or circumstances; which is positive and good! Therefore, love is the access and a gift to us all! And that is far beyond the cost of material possession, or any standard of the human faculties! This character, (LOVE) only leaved us with his will, to honor its power as a human race! And that's another way of gift, to allow our acknowledgement; come to submission, that's what equality is all about! The living of life is somewhat a decision through our choice we made! Collectively and individually.

The down fall from our emotions, coming through from pride. Our own selfish ways are a confusion from the negatives; Bam-baring against the positive! Not with understanding, but because of a misunderstanding. Not connecting, but because of disconnecting. Where there is no communication, its confusion.

SERENITY AND POWER

Where there is no peace, it's distressing. When there is no wisdom of the people, the nations are perishing! Show support to the spiritual side of life. Be InTouch with the divine connection. Have some quite times with yourself; so you can settle the core with others, and for yourself! Just by doing so, we are opening a channel for the positive. By allowing us to grow with great confidence. Building on our intelligence, of furthering the qualities of life future! Talking is easy, but acting is hard, but the qualities of life is depending on you. So therefore be true to yourself, because qualities are limitless! And real life worn the reflections from the qualities of our lives! We should be focusing on the level of qualities; we are portraying every day. As a results of our lives. Make no mistakes, we should connect ourselves. With courage and strength, love and the right environment of others. To be sustain by the positive! We should allow our conscience, to be our leader and guide; throughout the journey in our lives! Life is an open door of our future, and also its close the door of our destiny! The purposes of our lives enhance prosperity and happiness. Throughout our natural qualities, as we progress with our connection; within ourselves and towards others! Consider this in some-what ways, that we are keepers, rulers and protectors; through the wisdom, knowledge and understanding of the divine presence! Of the most entrusted one of our conscience, heart, minds and soul! The liberty of life is equal for everyone, and the ways we should share it! Is to learn how to appreciate each-others; as a part of the families, of the human race! We should exercise our understanding through the hands of communication. For the strength of peace to reign. For the gravity of life endures, and sustain in the eyes of love and courage. It is always good to face the circumstances, of our fears! But it's always hard to do so. But has human being we should always have prepared for the unexpected; we got to wise up ourselves, for any circumstances that may come our way. Life needs us, as to the positive connection from our minds! The vine, from which all powers comes from, confident should be the fruits of which we eat; to digest our minds focus, to a standard or level building our creditability! And our strength is to fight for victory, to overcome of what may surrounds us as obstacles! For no man is an island, we are together with the InTouch we face in life! By knowing that love is the gravity that show's us unconditional energy; spiritual energy!

Just think about this for a moment. We learn that there are eight planets revolves around the sun. As big as each of these planets are! Mercury, Venus, Earth and Mars, Jupiter, Saturn, Uranus and Neptune! Also consider the distance each planet is away from the sun! And the thousands of stars, we can see with our naked eyes. And the distance these galaxies are away from the blue sky? And the blue sky is one big covering over all the planets. There are hundreds' of thousand stars are distance away from each other's! Yet there are thousands of stars form the galaxy. The heavens are speaking to us, about unity. Collaboration of the human hearts on the positive! Is the glory of Love being of limitless measures? Just a little peak of our little imaginations. To the awesome purity of power, which brought all these elements to existence. How much does this says in questions. That there is nothing among these existing planets, is greater than life; because the divine life force is the source of these elements! The light of knowledge and understanding gave us a burning favor of the truth. A thrill to our hearts and minds. Allowing us to find hope and strength. The kind of sustaining power, from his divine presence; of whom is the source of all living things, as of nature! He who brings the natural beautification of our environment; without any material positions, or material distraction! This divine entity, of whom is the almighty of all creation. Has brings us glory and honor to our lives!

What is men as we see ourselves in our own eyes? Reckless and dishonest, deceiving has we are! And careless of whom we are in humanity. We lurk around poking in others personal affair. Thinking that it's all good, because our minds is seeing that negative shadows! As if something is real, as of beholding the truth. We can have deceived ourselves through our imaginations. Which seems so right that we can't resist! We should always understand that the right thing is real, different from the wrong! Has a human race, we can make matters gets worst. Through miscommunications, sometimes we are allowing ourselves. Following others in the gutter, pro-se. While leaders pretending to be wise, when they are fools! Remember one fool makes many fools. One bad apple spoils the whole bunch. It is embedded in most of our minds, that physical beauty can capture our attention! And made it becomes temptation. Most of us got their attention by having beautiful things. But I will send you this message that life is more than gold! We may can't change the things in the pass. But we can react to the present, to make a difference. When we engage ourselves to materiality! Any games can play to the insecurity of our lives. Life is a natural realistic evidence; and should identified where we need life to be. Despite of the evidences within our ups and downs. They say life is not fair, because we are not entrusted in the confidence of our self and others! We are still following the shadows of our imaginations; which keeping us on the edges of pride. Looking down on each other's, with a negative breath! Hoping the worst for our own flesh and blood.

Robert Francis

Together we can be strong with love and courage from within, has God bless the world…

MYSTIC ELEMENTS

Not knowing we are doing the evil to our own individual self. We are allowing the negative to conquer our heart. Not knowing that the darkness in evil is causing **a chain reaction.** Covering the whole world in devastation. And will make it harder for the nation to go back. Finding love, which is courage and strength, loyalty and peace, a divine purpose; the character of the positive! Who is the very presence of the almighty creator? The gift of life is given unto us to stand in the glory of his presence. We the generation should fight for each other's, as it is necessary within love! There is a light that is far beyond the sky; and yet so close to our hearts! A light that which holds the beauty and shapes our destiny. This light we describe to be the glorious energy is deep inside our souls.

UNITY IN REFLECTION

Which reflects our loyalty and integrity. It's the strength of consciousness and full awareness in our surroundings! It is evident that the children of the world needs unity. It's a legacy for humanity, a gift we should share in our circle. Unity is the very strength that keep us together. And once we denied this kind of character unity. We become totally ignorant in ourselves; and harmful to one another lives, not trusting within each one self! The target in love is missing from our hearts, soul and minds; because we are a distance away from loyalty. How can we received honor and find justice when there is no unity! Unity is one of the most powerful assets among the human race. We the people should open our eyes to the spiritual light; of true freedom towards ourselves! We have to look within our souls to find mercy upon others. As if we are in their place, in that moment in time. Love as already prepared a place for us! As others say God has prepared a place for us. And he will always there with us through the presence of life.

Remember this, be careful of the companies we keep! And the decision we made, in whatever circumstances it may be. We are to make God proud, from within one self; just like the Earthly father is proud of his son. Remember the famous saying! That a wise son makes a glad father. But a foolish son, is a burden to his mother! The human race should find love, blessings and wisdom with knowledge and understanding! To track in the conscious mind; it is all the source and purpose of our living. We should search for the truth, to strengthen our self and others! First in the circle of friendship; and Secondly, in the circle of stranger. For the innocent, the weak and the astray, and weary ones! I will draw our attention a little about character building! Has we payed attentions, with too many characters.

And famous men in the life of history? We would realize how important is to be born as babies, as a genetic code! Every person in life has a purpose. Has they keep grew-up has a person! Realizing the importance through life experiences. Has we transform from babies to adults. We should realize the transformation with the experiences. Has we taken responsibilities, taught by our family members! Parents, friends and teachers, and other people out there as we encounter. We took the responsibilities to build on our character! So we can be able to identify our purpose in **life.** There are many of us trying to work hard; wanted to identify such purpose that is there within. And to the value ourselves, and to allow the ability of management skill: to be a part of these circumstances of character building in our lives! Also many of us in the stage of our ability connections. In education, some of us we are less unfortunate educationally! But on the flip side of this, we can look on what we call common senses! Remember, we born with character; A raw material, within the senses of our ability. We capture from a different angle or circumstances in our lives! Where we came to surrender under the code of our ability connections. And stand up strong to face responsibilities. In whatever ways it shapes in our lives. For where it comes down to, is our life giver; of our spiritual strength! As to the generations in the pass and also present! Learn about the living God of creation our spiritual strength and maker! And some of these generations lost sight spiritually; and still losing that spiritual character! Where there is no knowledge in love, the people perishes! We can't find the way on our own, but as early as we can accept the wisdom of the Almighty God! We are good to go, with him on our side. He is the corner stone and foundation of our lives. That's an important character, of our character building! The Lord gave us the sight and strength: to face each day onward journey. He is the source we, will always fall on: and that is character when we allow ourselves to. Our courage and determination, the love and loyalty, peace and mercy that's character! And all of this coming from the source of life, the creator! And his character, made it worthwhile for living! How can we see the power of the almighty God; when we have no vision? Our spiritual vision is blindfold by the philosophy of the world. The vengeance of men came from their own ignorance! And the frustrated, agitated lives, is of their negative minds. The father of lies, who is the devil doesn't want to take the blame of his destructiveness!

REVELATIONS

So he came up with a society world plan. So he can escape in the secret of his delusions! Through the era of this revolution; generations must come to acknowledge the reality of their lives! By knowing that freedom in love. Love is the most powerful assets! Which is the present of God Almighty. His presence taught us to learn from each other's! By the hands of his righteousness, through the eyes of his mercy, forgiveness and loyalty, which brings us to another step! Which is dignity, the power that enhance freedom by love. When Christ blood spilt on the cross, it was a seal, to establish the power of forgiveness. Through God's love in Christ our saviour! When we holding back, not to forgive. We are giving power to the enemies. For we allow the enemies themselves, to rationalized the situations in our head. Then behind our backs, they say that we are a fools!

DELUSIONS

How could this person have done you this wrong? And you thinking of forgiving this person! Get your revenge from this circumstances.

The enemy is prompting you to do evil. Better yet, the enemy put someone in your life! To enforces the negatives in you. But of course you don't see that you are blindfold by deceptions. Because all is in your mind! Is that, he or she was wrong to say or did such wrong to me! And you think you have the rights still, by revenging. No, you don't have any more of that rights. The enemy trick you, and you losing power to that rights of liberty! In such circumstances of emotional connection. Until then, if you are not feeling a sense of isolation and disconnection from the truth! You still with a close mind, not responding to the spirit of the Most High God! The conscience which is the spirit of God should high light within us! The circumstances or conditions which surrounds us. Should reflects our consciousness, in knowledge and wisdom. Until we free ourselves from emotional stress. Through the glory and strength from forgiveness. Has we eyes it up and size it up. To make a difference in one's life! Can we see how love is pure? Love is a purge; love can take away your pain! And give you happiness again. Yes, we should always consider the good Qualities of our partners. What is it that keep us going with our relationship? The same thing with Almighty God! What are the Qualities keeping us going with the lord? Love and forgiveness never fail. Love covers the multitude of sins. Love is loyalty and total honesty. In every given circumstances at hand! So come clean, and try to be honest. And love will find your heart, soul and mind! Love will bring to your peace and contentment.

I can have assured you, that by redefining yourself; is allowing yourself to be unwrap by the Holy Spirit from the father of creation! You see, when you denied life. The same, life denied you. Because life is of the Holy Spirit, who is the character of God! Who open all of your settings to you? Such as wisdom, knowledge and understanding, which sustain by love. Which gives peace through the experience of contentment! Be more aware what the power of darkness can do to your life! So you don't have to walk through darkness. The light is a beauty, which keep our lives healthy and strong. I don't think many of us ever think about life this way; that we don't own this life, we are just a keeper of life! But through the spiritual wisdom of the master. He gave us the tools to guard and protects life, and nourishing it. So when we are feeling pain or someone tries to harm us! We do whatever it takes to shield ourselves from the harm and pain. And it's a human natural reaction doing so! Therefore, we intent to raise up a flag. Not to trust such person or things which tried to harm us or to cause us pain! But here is the thing, by the acknowledgement of the almighty God presence. Through his wisdom with understanding! It's the tools which he gave us to the power of forgiveness, through the circumstances! That we continue the connection with each other's. Knowing to the fact that we are not perfect! When we done someone wrong, or someone done you wrong. Then we disconnect ourselves, of trusting in that someone. Then it's like our whole world is in disconnection! Each person to another, which in fact that where we are heading! And as a result, we are perishing. Not trusting or communicating anymore! But the strength of forgiveness would take us to a different prospective. By giving freedom additionally to our lives! By reviewing the circumstances of the damages which had done! We have to allow the power of forgiveness to take control in our circumstances! To free up our hearts, soul and minds. By allowing the blessing of joy, peace, love and happiness. To kick in from the power of the master's glory! We are not the owner of this life, but just the keeper. Nevertheless, we should work together collectively as one human race! We should also know that time changes things. So is also prayers changes things! As times travel we grow within the experiences of ourselves. And the experiences of yourself to others! Then we feel and see the broadening and the arising of intelligence in the circle of our lives! The strength of unification magnified our ability through the love of the master! So we can see much more of the values of love.

LOYALTY IS STRENGTH

Of what forgiveness can do, for our freedom in life. Let me ask you a question. What is it, about a construction zone? Hypothetically, when you see a construction zone. You are thinking of repairing or rebuilding! Something falls down or broken apart. Sometimes when you are in your car driving. Everything is around you looking great. Having good weather excellent speed in your driving! And as soon as you see the sign says construction zone. First thought is speed check. And secondly you are having a setback on your journey. Of getting to your destiny! At sometimes rough spots and narrow areas you experience in driving. In some places of construction zone. There is long line of traffic! You might as well give up hope. Of getting to your destiny in time! There you become anxious, frustrated and agitation; riding up from everywhere in your head! Patient is getting lesser and lesser uncontrollable. Everyone in the moment of the traffic line, is not doing so well stuck in the construction zone! Our minds and feelings can get work up in the times of troubles!

Think for a few moments, you having construction zone in your life! Sometimes brokenness is hard crossing. And unrepair bridge still in our lives! It's like traffic of obstacles, in the area of our construction zone. When we are experiencing agony and pains! But the repairer is not there yet. We need to invites him to our hearts. To reconstruct our broken bridge. To repair our trials and tribulations, our sad hearts and pains! What happens when the waves of uncertainty under our bridge? It's creeping up in our hearts, and minds! The construction zone of our lives needs to be repair. By the repairer! We are talking about the best man in town, we need to find! The one who do a good job. The one who also leaved a good reputation. We would like that repairer who stand behind his works, words and character! The one who can repair's our hearts, soul and minds. He always leaved a trail of love, and peace, joy and happiness from his foot prints! So that the helpless, weak and innocent can follow a way of his foot prints to find him! When the chief foreman gives orders. To all the work men on the construction site. To carry out their potential post, of what they should be doing for the cause of the repairing! So is our master, the Father of creation. The Most High God of our lives. His spiritual hands make a great deal in our lives. He has orders his angels to carry out their potential post. Accordingly, to their abilities, to what zone the master will send them! To repair the heart of the lonely. And for those who's going through agony, sadness and pain. Some having no food to eat or clean water to drink! Angels speaks and acts in the authority of the master's Holy Spirit! And also the creator uses us has humanity. To help shouldering the burdens of others. Which helps us to stay connected under his holy power. And that which I describe as Love and courage! We are keepers for one another. And the strength to embrace the weak. The wise, speaks to the negative hearts. Wherein loyalty rebuke dishonesty. Knowledge is for the ignorant. Understanding makes the humble strong! We all have a construction zone in our lives. Which needs repairing. By reconstruct the circumstances, which involves in our hearts, soul and minds! We all needs the Most High God in our lives. Who is all wise, who is all perfect, and so ever sure about his reputation? That will never go dim, in the sight of our presence. We can live the master's happiness. And stand in the presence of his glory.

Make no mistakes about Jehovah words. There is no turning back on his words. Which is the strength and prosperity of our lives! God Almighty never fail in his works. And his love never gets mess up! He is as pure has his Love, and his Love is as pure as him! He has no character differences. He is as natural, as natural could be. If we want victory, we seek neutrality, with a sound conscious heart! {Detachment of partiality in the objectives}. Unity will draw us closer and closer, and as we know confidence is with the competent. Release yourselves from the darkness of the negatives! And stand up by taken a glimpse in the light. To see the truth in prosperity and happiness, freedom and love! Because unification as a big part to play in our lives. If we can open our soul to the truth. In agreement with one to the other! We can have a great fulfillment in our lives of freedom. Through the pureness of love, unity as a small figure!

But the character of unity, step like giant; accompany with loyalty, hope and faith! Treading the road of Righteousness. A man who is pure and true, thinking for the benefits of others! And not for the benefits of his own self. That man should able to look in the eyes of another man. To know if he is trust worthy or not. The strength of unity has a strong sense of energy and urgency, with patience! Unconditional love invited unification to be a part of his works. Why I say his, because love is God, whose image is in the image of man! Throughout all of these positive characters, such as first the Holy Spirit. Within the integrity of loyalty, purity, kindness, and humility.

GENEROSITY

We should have the sense of oneness towards humanity! So that generations after generations can carried the light of God's glory.

To everlasting through eternity! The strength of God's Love clothing with unification, stand in the arising of his people. For the man who live good for the benefits of tomorrow's future! His legacy is of eternity, for many are unfold. Through the knowledge of his loyalty towards humanity! The king of glory will come in to the hearts and minds of the humble. Who is the king of glory, the Most High who is strong and mighty! He who have the army of thousands and ten thousands of Angels. He is the king of glory, and Omnipotent in his power! The presence of the Most High covers all the spectrum in his kingdom power! Or is to say, God's power and presence. Stretches beyond the boundaries of men thoughts or imaginations. Think about it for a while, the Almighty God is the spirit of life himself! What other boundary is there hidden? That the wisdom of God is not yet discover! Can men come to that kind of thoughts? Whom life was given unto them! We the generation came to existence. Only to discover the wisdom and knowledge of the Most High God! And try to find the part way to happiness and prosperity. And the great consoler of our lives! Teaches us how to use the tools getting to the road of happiness! We should open our eyes, and look within ourselves! By seeing the truth in the light of righteousness. In which the great God of life plan the ways for our lives. We are truly design in the uniqueness of his wisdom! We the human race are on top of his list. For the unity purposes. God said love your neighbors as you love yourself. Why? Bear with me, I quote again. He said do unto others, as you would like them do unto you! First loving yourself is a very good step! In experiencing how to show love to others. And doing positively and unconditionally! You will earn the respect from others, to love you the way you are deserved to be love! Keep remind yourself the importance of life. Because the Almighty God he is of the living. That's why you are alive, for the spirit of life who is God, Is in you! That's a statement Jehovah the creator has made right there. That we all, are his master piece! So, can't you see that we the human race who respect God Almighty! Come to set layers after layers in the glory of his mighty work. By his wisdom through generation after generations! Can anyone say when his works will end? He is everlasting to everlasting, to generations unto generations! The more we can teach our kids how to unite. Within one self and also to others. What a great place the levity of humanity will be, in the respect of God and men! We have to build our confident in relation to the Father of our heavens! He lives within us; we have to certify that knowledge! Because the Father of creation have no hiding place from his people. And you my friend should have hope and faith, in his mercy! The same way this society world of this political strategy! Unite through the generations of politicians, and still uniting! As back in the days of King Nebuchadnezzar, and his son Belshazzar! And way back before these men political power. And the unification of these political lineage! Now here I ask the question. What about the generations who love God! We should spread more vividly, to the power of his glory! With love unconditionally, gently, loyally, intelligently and untiringly!

INDEPENDENCE IN RIGHTEOUSNESS

The power of the Almighty, is naturally independent with spiritual freedom. We should learn to be grateful, for everything in life! Yes, sometimes the good transform from the bad experiences.

Bottom line, we have to be determine and be strong! Through the consciousness, and the positive ways of our lives. We should be thankful for our parents, for trying their best. Teaching us Godliness through the tough times in our lives! Teaching us how to love each other's in unity. And for been thankful to the Almighty God! For the tendency of our parents! Amongst us as brothers and sisters. A tribute from us, Pastol, Freda, Raphael, Rob, Tyrone, Dimple, Oswald, Donald and Ashley! A loving memory of our parents, who teaches us; to have love and respect through tough times! We all should be thankful in general to our parents in loving memories. We should have a reunion parent's day! To spread the power of respect and love to our parents! As we enhance our roots through our lineage of generations. We should rise over the mountains of agony and struggling! And become champions in of our lives. The future depends on us through the powers of the Almighty God. As to the spirit of life, who is God Himself? The purity of Love, never otherwise describe defeat to our future! Or in any way show partiality, through his character! I said his, because love is God. And God Almighty is the spiritual eyes on our journey! If we allow him to play that important part in our lives. Just the way our parents allowed him to. Just think about it for a while, having yourself so bless! By having one foot in the door, pre-se! Just to have a little taste of the Holy Spirit wisdom! What more else would we be thankful for. As a protection through this dark world of vanity life! Simple, the Most High God is saying. Life is beautiful to be thankful for. And Satan, the Devil, the father of deception! Is saying that vanity is beautiful to be thankful for! But my question is, if you don't have life! How are you going to be thankful for anything? So which is the first you should be thankful for? So now you can see where our roots are coming from. It's through the rightful hands of God Almighty wisdom. Down to our parents, generations after generations. As the Holy Spirit naturally empowered those who intended to be wise! The humbleness from our hearts! Lean to the higher calling of wisdom, knowledge and understanding. The philosophy of the Master's Holy Spirit changes characters. That's why we could go back to say thanks, to our parents! Generations after generations, throughout the Nations. Appreciation is a beautiful strength to humanity! We the human race should hold strong to the reality and morality. As the corner stone, of what Love can do! For our future generations, has we saw the great things; Love has done in the past, reaching for greater golds. Breaking down barriers, bringing down mountains and to free those in the valleys! Has we keep hearing that soft still voice within! Saying give love a chance, to burn away the negative! Let the positive come fill that gap, and take you back to the place! In the Garden of Eden, we are talking freedom. You see my friend, love as a vision. And is a vision, for our lives! Jehovah the great Master wanted, and intend to bring us victory. It's good over evil, life over death, light over darkness and righteousness over sin! Is it ever occurred to you that we can find a cure for happiness? Instead of you using drugs to get high. God in his glory, through the

SIZE IT UP AND EYES IT UP.

WISDOM POWER

Holy Spirit of his wisdom! Can bring us to that place, feeling high, tremendously high! As if we are walking on clouds, feeling good in great confidence. In most cases, seeing the evil before it come and hit you in the face. What more high you want to get? When you are highly protected under the power of his Majesty! The one of whom, who teaches us humbleness and how to forgive one another. Our Father use to teach us these lines of verses from the Bible. Its goes on to say, little children love each other's! Never cause each other's pain. But if your brother speaks in anger, answer not in wrought again! He said, for this is the power! For soft answers turn away wrought. But grievous words strived up anger! Forgiveness has the power to release freedom of oneself, and for others! Please don't be selfish with that calling. You will end up hurting yourself, and others. Until you open your minds to the truth! For evil have no significance in its power, bringing happiness to life. Or in no wise reward any quality of peace! Darkness, is for the light to shine through. To erase the dark, the dark cannot erase the light. The light is for you to see the way of consciousness. And the dark is for you to stumble, through struggles doing wrong things! And can cause a whole lot of pain and agony, disrespect and sadness. Also with courage and determination, can rescue you out of darkness of the struggles of disloyalty! As to the light of Love will receive in you; as a result of happiness and prosperity, spiritually. The wonders of love light, will representing you has a new creature! Spiritually and emotionally, as the stepping stone of divine wisdom, Knowledge and understanding; shaping the path ways for our lives. We can shout with confident by the testing of faith and hope. That we have found victory, from his majesty. Through his love, mercy and grace in abundancy to everlasting to everlasting!

The Almighty glory will grow in the heart of men. As a legacy to all generations. And the redeemer will reveal his presence to nations in all walks of life! Regardless the colors, class or creek, his unfolding love will see us through our endeavor! We are inspired by the spirit of the Lord. Has we been taught to hang on with loyalty, for honesty is a beauty! It's a substance that sustain life, with character. Sharing is a unifying strength which helps life to grow! Once we are walking with a sober mind; we will find connections from each other's. As rewarding to humanity for power and strength! Love brings us to surrender under the beautification of happiness naturally. How can we see the light, through our spiritual eyes! First, we have to exercise our commitment. Looking through the handy works, and promises of the Most High God! The stars, the moon and sun and of the whole heavens. Ask yourself this question, how all of these could be in existence; without an everlasting power? Just by take a peek into that intriguing window of the Almighty Creator! You will start to feel a little spiritual connection, in your heart! Love is abounding with wisdom, the respect and fear of the great Master, of everlasting life! His Omnipotent and Omnipresent has keep us sustaining. All through the days of our lives, through the struggles and temptations! And also through the good times of us glorifying the excellences of the Most High God. When I look to see the secrets in the existence of life. The only thing I could came up with, is love! Why love, why it couldn't be something else than love?

LOVE AS ONLY COMMITMENT

Because love is the real identity of God. Whose kingdom is a holy everlasting kingdom! Also when we view through the existence of life. Within the characters of all these great men, who fight for liberation! For the weak and the innocent ones. These great men are ones who deeply understand, been through the valleys. Of struggling, pain and abuse! Through the eyes of tribulation, was interpreted as going through the fire to be purified! Because when each day rises. It's about going through moments of survival. For everything which points at these great men! Was a season to their everyday life of living, they went through! Has their continuation carrier on with their character building? These men became more transform with spiritual strength! And as other great men became more connected. Through the works of other characters, within the stages and level of their commitment! The love of Almighty God sees them safely through! Fighting for the poor, weak and innocent ones. Has they keep on invites their sober minds. To take more roots in their lives, giving them strength! And upliftment with the ability of their changing characters. Their love and consideration became more deeply for others of humanity! Building a wall of protection for others consistently. Having that conscious conversation; building a relationship of spiritual consciousness! For others like the weak, poor and the innocent. To build their spiritual destiny, and grow with the spiritual revelation! For the destiny of mankind, is about spiritual consciousness; love and unity!

The power of love from the heavenly father. Raising the bars in the light and true meaning, for civilized power in humbleness! That a great meaning when nations can come together. Through the strength and connection of communication. All true perspectives are character building through the eyes of wisdom, knowledge and understanding! And which these are the roots from where all these uprising intellectual sense of energy came from. Which are so naturally, and humbly establish justly! As the courage and love of the Almighty authentically and patiently. Slowly emerge with great reflection right before the human race. Or before this great nation on planet earth! We should come to submission in love. Mother planet earth, is in her beautification shines through the landscape of her character. Sending out her loving energy in her produce. Such as fruits, foods, vegetation and within all other nature in lives! Amongst the human race, love the greatest character represent God Almighty. And the signature of the Most High One. And love the Omnipotent and Omnipresent, in all of his entity! Who is God Almighty, the living of the living? Love is his greatest energy and a true light amongst the humanity on planet earth! The unquestionable Jehovah, Glorious in Holiness and fearful in praises. He is of his own independent existence. And his signature is love in every step form and shape! The level of the Almighty is fathomless. And remain uniquely untouchable character! His Holy presence in love, as a true sense of direction and protection! And courage is to deliver. Loyalty is to show care and share. Wisdom is to honor and fear. Knowledge is to open the light, and to reveal what's in the dark. And understanding is to keep all objectives organize; in the presence of his Holy Spirit! Of whom is the most high in full circles, in his majesty? But we all totally come short of his glory of his righteousness! But yet, we the human race has considered uniquely his image, and master piece! For through us his image shines. His holy spirit speaks through us, as he is intended of his power! But has we all committed searching for the light of his power. The truth of righteousness begins to reveals. Becoming more humble to the true light. Our sense of connection begins to experiencing the sense of values. As a tread to cross over to the side of God in his **righteousness!** It's an experiences of struggles, agony and pain. As a testing to our faith through hoping to find soberness of our minds! Which brings us to a sense of justice and satisfaction. Searching for happiness and prosperity! The strength of hope is a companion with faith. As in sometimes we keep asking for mercy and forgiveness. Has he look into our circumstances, we plea for our cause in the light of his love! So according to his mercy, we can be blessed by his presence in our lives! Has we keep on communicating and keep connecting, as people. As a nation, and as planet earth. Our calling is our deepest responsibilities from one to the other; because no one stands alone, we are all keepers! The Almighty puts us here to work with him, and his Angels! Has he spread his glory through us? Lord lead us, please leads us through the valleys! Please carry us between the mountains with your blessings. We ask you for faith and hope; we ask you to inspire us through your eyes. And to fulfill your destiny in us. Please let your forgiveness set us free. Cause your eyes to be the light in us, so we can see. Cause us not to keep wondering through the mountains!

SPIRITUAL APPRECIATIONS

But to have hope and faith in you. Our endeavor is very great, we alone cannot find the solutions by ourselves! We ask for your merciful hands, to be with us. All through the days of our lives, father of Abraham! There are many of us, who never feel happiness. Or to experience prosperity. I know we are often attack by the negative energy in various ways. We are not conscious of a sober mind. Calculating what could be the results from our actions! You see my friend, just by coming to a point of understanding. How to listen to that soft still voice of wisdom, speaking to you. We all have to adopt within ourselves. Committing ourselves analyzing the difference between good and bad! Between the positive and the negative. We have to learn how to feel the energy when it's good or bad. By practice faith, and learn to be patient in hope. Slowly take actions, so you can experience results leads to satisfaction! It takes a lots of courage within us, to connect with the love of God. So that we can commit ourselves more to the positive! By so doing, the blessing of the great redeemer. Will enriching us prosperously! It's the true light we see, in the Master's eyes. Set us apart as unique and special through the eyes of his wisdom. The heavenly in his highest, reveals to our ability. His positive energy, a class unlike the other. Teaches the stages of power, and courage reflecting his values! That when the Odds is against you. Is to remember that Almighty God will always love you. Because is his strength that take you out of every given situation. He always there through the presence of his wisdom. He is the chief of understanding. And the Master of knowledge. And he is also the founder of wisdom. And the anchor of faith with hope.

ONE AND ONLY TRUE MASTER

The only legend of loyalty, the Father of peace and mercy! His holy presence is forgiveness and Love! What can we say, about the Most High integrity and dignity? It is the very footprint which we follows through our lives! To received his blessings and prosperity. So let us stand strong, while we hold his cards in our hands! Many of us through the era of time, displayed the living of our lives. We have been listening to the wrong voice inside our head.

The negativities of all kinds of deceptions spread its wings. Through the eyes of Lucifer, the father of deceptions! Our imagination draws us closer to his deceptive power. Has we open our minds calculating within the shadow, of a reflection; of what seems to be real! But unconsciously we are covers under a shadow of things, which is not sustainable! Let us open our eyes to the truth. Allow our heart and soul to experience the chances of standing on solid ground! We are swept off our feet, to the path of destruction. Wrong calculations to life, can result us disasters. Like family confusions, negative response from friends! Disagreement from one another. Generational war, nation war against nation. Envy and strive, gossips, sabotaging, penalizing. That's what the results of deception do to our lives. And there are so much more, behind the power of deception. We have to invite love and courage to enter our lives! Which give us a positive energy, in hope and faith. Has we surrender ourselves in commitments for our lives. We have to come to the border of decision. Or on the other side of the river. To behold the bright true light, which inviting love to come into our hearts and minds! So we can share mercy and courage. To help connects all nation, generation, people and person! Under the power of unification, within oneself. And has we feel the trust begins to flows; through the heart of the human race! With the strength of life, the eyes of the Most High God connecting within us! We should make up our minds, and let him be our greatest comforter! And friend to lead the way, of our life journey. As to the inspiration to our destiny. My brothers, sisters, and friends. For all the tough experience in our lives. Often happens as a results, when we following the shadows of darkness. Which cause our back against the wall. In other words, when we fall. Or end up finding ourselves between the rock and a hard place! It's about time now. To commit ourselves to the truth which can allows our lives to be in peace! To be content, we are talking about spiritual freedom. I will say this again. To be sober minded, it takes a lots of courage, love, faith, wisdom, mercy and forgiveness! Which brings prosperity and happiness into our lives. Just by allowing the Omnipresent and the Omnipotent one in our lives! All these attributes, is the richness of our legacy. As a blessing from the Almighty to be happy. We the human race should not allow ourselves, under the enslavement of deception! Then we eventually will become the bad apple amongst the good apples!

A PRAYER

Good Lord we thank you in appreciation of your Love and courage. From your great wisdom, as you lend us your mercy. Through the power of your loyalty in spiritual knowledge and understanding! Your forgiveness as open the door of freedom for our lives! We give you honor and praise for your Omnipotent unique image! That you keep reflecting on us, your people. Your love is one which keep us in safety. Through the obedience and humbleness of your Angel. Lord, your intelligence has captured the power of your kingdom the true light. Your elegancy has captured the beauty of your radiance, in your holiness. Your glory has surrender the cause of your Righteousness. We thank you for the good hearted around us. As fragile as life may seems to be, you brought us through the fire without getting burn! You gave us strength to build, brick by brick, and stick by stick. You just allow many of us to accomplish obstacles! Through the journey of our lives. Thanks Eternal Father for my destiny and journey. You just help me to accomplish. You are the greatest blessing to this world, and also planet earth! Amen…

OUR JOURNEY

We the nation should capture the shadow, of this image! Which is the image of the living God Almighty! The founder of wisdom and Love. A positive energy that he uses to interact with his people of the human race. Through generations after generations. We should hold strongly to the ties of his spiritual energy of forgiveness. That he shares with us, has we join hands in hands from our hearts and soul! To bring an earthly peace, of a changing world. Paradise, where prosperity shines. A planet, where mankind come to connects in communication of loyalty. We are weary travelers, journeying a long way to our destiny! Each one needs, company. To converse with others enjoying the journey. Happiness give us strength, when we are forsaken. We need love and understanding to build our future. Every man should reflect on their dream, as we link from one to the other. We should learn how to enjoy this dream that should never be broken! Has step by step, we planet earth learn the spiritual treat. How to sincerely lean on one another for the better of our future. Life depending on our future. And our future is a dreaming block, we secure for prosperity! And as peace and happiness, becomes the cup and Saucer. Which enhance love to life happiness! We the human race should be more secure, has flesh and bones. Let us stop the bloodshed, life is the meaning for the living. This is a message to the world, let's stop being ignorant to the positive! The truth we must learn to face; and we should learn to share our destiny on common ground! Let us admit that love is our heart beat. If we don't start to look deep within. There will be a passage in time, when darkness of catastrophe; will spread the human hearts uncontrollable, without mercy! The more the truth reveal its colors! The disturbance, of the world is acting up!

Let's respect and honor life to the max. You think vanity is the substance of life? Is not everything shines like diamond is real! Be careful of how you feel. Our lives are a raw deal, is a gift of righteousness to seal. We can't stray away from the wisdom of the Most High. He is the leader and faith of our lives. And a comforter on our life journey. What is there to lose, trusting in the wisdom of the father? I must say this to you all. Take a look around you, and tell me what you see. We are people, a nation, a family, human being, flesh and bones, an image of a natural movements! We are not aliens. Absolutely not, the only way we should describe as an aliens!

LOVE CONQUERS

Is if we have, and carrying hatred in our hearts. Against our own human flesh and bones on this planet earth. Love conquers all things, and prayer brings us humbleness. To see that the answers changes all things! Love is life and the substance of life, how can we prosper without love! The compassion, the mercy, faith and loyalty, in happiness! All is from love, if you allow yourself to the integrity of love. Love will become your warrior to fight the darkness of hate and evilness for you. Just find the vision and strength of humbleness, to lean on love! Many of us think that we are foolish to have love in our hearts. They said that we are weak and soft in foolishness. But love can cut the bars of iron in struggles, emotional pain. And give you strength to sustain. Love can erase the passage of evil tidings. And bring togetherness to all humanity. And burn away all cruelties out of our lives! We just have to listen to the voice within. And to follow through with the right imaginations. We should be strong to have love. When we see love and peace, we should never crush it. Then if we do, it would be the beginning of destruction for our lives! Love transpires and inspired the intelligence of our hearts! When we breathe the air, it's the same as smell the atmosphere. That the way we should honor love, in the sense of honoring someone! As supposedly honoring yourself and the Almighty Father.

HONOR!

Each person should stand up for justice. When there is justice to stand up for. To respect ourselves has God creation. We all should be in full recognition to the importance of our lives… happiness stand for what it means. Never will let us down.

Come to the table of honor within one self. By seeing the beauty our actions. For in the future, those who seems to be our enemies. Will still have a conscience to whisper our names; for goodness sake! When they tried to befall us over and over. Get up, rise again, and Let them see what the strength is, in **us**. As to the power of our integrity! As nation, and as people in our own cultures and tongues. We should find stability, with power and strength. Intelligence to capture our souls through serenity!

FACING REALITY

Think about this for a while. In life we are like a chain to its links. Every fellow men are a keeper, to his own fellow men! We are helpers, servants and keepers of one another. Never will anyone accomplish anything by her or himself. We always need a helping hand. You can't sail the ship by yourself. While you are in the center, you will need someone to set up the sails for the wind! Has you keep directing the ship, you need others; to provide other services for you! Its calls company, people connects together as one! That's why love is so essential for life. Love is the actual nostril which energized life, through generations after generations! We the people of the world, should stop the aggression of oppression; Let us overcome the power struggles. And controlling power over one's mind. Live for the beautification and justification with compassion. Let love find its course through our hearts; like rivers run to the sea, causing our conscience to be free! In humility amongst humanity. This planet Earth has a nation fill with pride. To bring our good deeds under one umbrella of intelligence! Our journey is narrow, as to the ups and down we face. Almighty Father we thank you. For giving us the strength of visions and inspiration in communication. Sustain us with courage and love, perseverance. Has we hold the control of our destiny. Through happiness and prosperity! Bless us as a people, a nation and family. So we can inherit your glory for generations to come; to experience your everlasting kingdom. Amen!

www.ingramcontent.com/pod-product-compliance
Lightning Source LLC
Chambersburg PA
CBHW071502070526
44578CB00001B/413